To Be an Indian

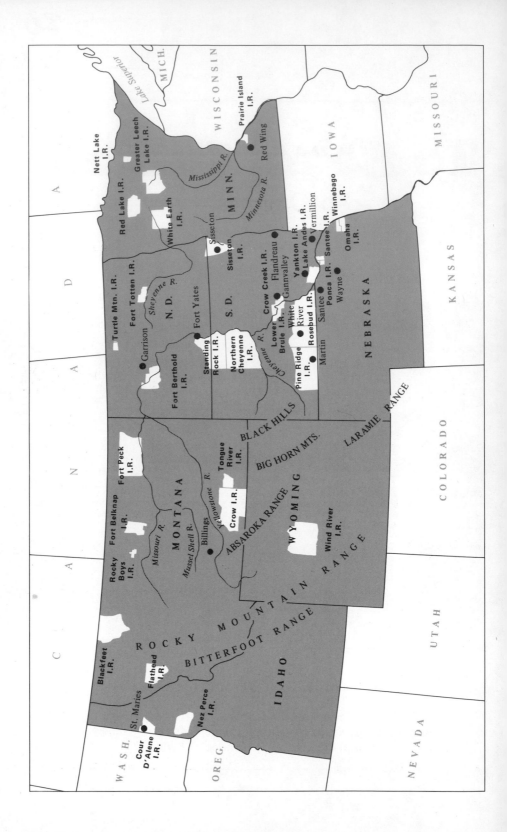

To Be an Indian

An Oral History

Edited by
Joseph H. Cash

and
Herbert T. Hoover

HOLT, RINEHART AND WINSTON, INC.
New York   Chicago   San Francisco   Atlanta   Dallas
Montreal   Toronto   London   Sydney

This book is dedicated
to Miss Doris Duke
A true friend of the Indian Americans

Acknowledgments

The editors wish to extend appreciation to Professor Ramon Harris and to Marki Peterson, both members of the American Indian Research Project staff, for enormous contributions in processing, organizing, and editing the materials that follow. General Lloyd Moses of the Institute of Indian Studies at the University of South Dakota was most helpful during the collection of the material. Acknowledgment must be made for the useful criticisms and encouragement of Paul Prucha, Marquette University, Milwaukee, Wisconsin; N. Scott Momaday, University of California, Berkeley; and Bea Medicine, San Francisco State College. We offer deep appreciation for steadfast encouragement by our wives, Margaret Cash and Karolyn Hoover. Above all, we are grateful to the marvelous Indian people who helped us always with graciousness and hospitality.

Foreword

The editors of this book have accomplished a unique piece of work that was a revelation to me. In interviewing "all sorts and conditions of men" among the Indian people, they have used a method that is fully American Indian. The white man knows from his experience during the past several centuries that in conferring with the Indians much time is consumed. Why? Because it is the American Indian way to discuss subjects so that any tribal member who wishes may have opportunity to express himself. Nothing is ever decided without the full knowledge of everyone. I rejoiced in reading this splendid book to see that the editors have got their material in this utterly democratic way.

I would ask that readers keep in mind what I have tried to say. If these narratives are to make an impression upon their lives, they should remember that "all sorts and conditions" of Indian people have expressed themselves to produce this literature.

FATHER VINE DELORIA
Vermillion, South Dakota

Preface

For centuries, Europeans and Americans have been writing histories of American Indians. They have studied them, invaded their privacy, and cast theoretical concepts about their image, their past, their future, and their psyche. Through all this activity, few thought to ask the Indians themselves about their past, and even fewer made any attempt to show the history of these great people through their own eyes.

In 1966, Miss Doris Duke, long concerned with the problems of Indian people, let it be known in academic circles that she was willing to support efforts to gather "Indian history from the Indian point of view." It was her hope that through the use of the technique of oral history Indian information and perspective could be gathered and disseminated.

Among the several institutions responding to the challenge was the University of South Dakota. The American Indian Research Project organized and began field research among the numerous tribes of the Northern Plains in the summer of 1967. Since that time, the research has been constant, and more than 800 separate interviews have been placed in the University archives. This collection, when combined with the collections of the six other Duke projects, provides unparalleled source material on American Indian history.

The South Dakota project has used certain guidelines for the collection of its oral interviews. The interviewer had to discover as much as possible about the subject matter and the people before he began working, in order to gain the utmost in depth and clarity from his informants. He was to avoid becoming too rigid, and thereby unnecessarily restricting the flow of information concerning subjects that might not be of primary interest to him but that could prove vital to someone else. Above all, he was not to "lead" the informant by injecting too much of himself into the finished product. Whether the researchers succeeded must ultimately be decided by the reader.

Serious scholars are aware that oral history, while it has great value, has limitations. The accuracy of a man's memory may diminish with time. Stories retold over a span of decades have a way of altering themselves in an unintended manner. Each narrative is the view of a single man, and what he sees may be entirely different from the way another sees the same thing from a different vantage point. Because of these factors, scholars must employ all their critical faculties if they are to use oral history properly. They must balance the oral testimony with other types of material. If they do this, they will find that these interviews offer them new subjects, and new insights, that have never before been available.

College students who are assigned this book as a supplement to a course in history, anthropology, or political science may be somewhat aghast to discover that no one has interpreted the material for them. Such persons should be cautioned by the advice given scholars, but they should be encouraged, too. Here they will find the raw material of scholarship unmuddied by the personal opinions of editors. They will be free and unfettered in forming judgments, seeking motivations, and formulating theories of their own.

General readers will find that these pages have not solved the "Indian problem" for them, but rather have exposed it for more careful consideration. Here can be discovered pathos, humor, serious thought, and visions of both the past and the future. The Indian people who speak from these pages are not the sullen, apathetic figures portrayed by so many; nor are they the glittering, plumed warriors of the motion picture and television screens. They are contemporaries. Few of the words written here were uttered more than four years before their printing. The Indians speaking are articulate, thoughtful, concerned, and informed citizens of the United States, telling it as it appeared from the latter 1960s. The reader may agree with some and disagree with others, but he cannot ignore any of them. These are their words, and this is their book.

In the first section, "Things that Guide the People," they speak of spiritual life and folklore. Indians of the Northern Plains region have deep-rooted spiritual traditions. Over thousands of years they have developed their own beliefs regarding the creation of the world and the origin of man, and they have designed unique ways to approach God—Wakantanka. They have prayed in steamy sweat lodges; and they have sought visions through fasting. The vision quest has taken many forms. Some have sat in sweat lodges; some have stood on hilltops holding peacepipes toward Heaven. Some have been lashed to the ground; others have engaged in the Sun Dance. Through all these means, they have sacrificed and suffered to catch glimpses of God's will for use in resolving the problems of this world. In modern times the old traditions persist, but they have competition. Christianity has lured some away. Indian organizations of recent vintage have drawn off others—the Native American Church, for example. The intrusion of new sects and denominations has not altered their spiritual orientation, however; American Indians remain deeply religious.

They also cherish a large volume of knowledge carried along in stories by word of mouth. Some relate to moral principles; others provide enjoyment. Together they comprise the literature of the tribes.

In the second section of the text, "Reservation Life," the informants speak of the years when Indians were forced to accept reservations during the nineteenth and early in the twentieth centuries, as people of European extraction seized their lands. This confinement imposed a revolution in life-style. For the adults, it meant the surrender of a life of hunting, gathering, and limited planting, and the acceptance of any available alternatives. Some cut wood; a few hauled supplies for the United States Army. Many took up farming; a limited number left the reservations to join the "dominant society." For the children, confinement on reservations meant enrollment in schools. Through the reservation period, most of them attended either Indian boarding or day schools, where they were regimented and forced to accept "white man's culture" at the expense of their own. For old and young alike, the whole experience was traumatic. The final interview in this section reveals that the result was demoralization, and sometimes moral decay.

The third section, "Depression, War, and a Revival of Self-Government," describes the road to recovery. Confinement on reservations had left Indians without land. Their education was, for the most part, of poor quality, and their health was neglected. Their political systems were confused, and their values were threatened. At least, this was the picture painted in a survey submitted by the Institute for Government Research at the request of the Secretary of the Interior in the late 1920s. In response, Commissioner of Indian Affairs, John Collier, offered a "new deal" to Indians, which any tribe could accept or reject in popular referendum. Some tribes rejected the offer, but more accepted it. And for those who accepted the "new deal," there came a reversal of the policies forced upon them over the two previous generations. The Wheeler-Howard Act (Indian Reorganization Act) of 1934 afforded them self-government and new business opportunities. Other related laws provided extension of the land base and educational opportunities in public schools, along with other advantages.

Meanwhile, they received New Deal relief benefits. The CCC (Civilian Conservation Corps), the WPA (Works Progress Administration), and the myriad of agencies that brought food to non-Indians during depression years were extended onto reservations. The plight of most Indians was improved noticeably.

Soon, certain New Deal benefits were withdrawn. When World War II broke out, the Government terminated relief on the premise that full employment would accompany the war. This did not happen on reservations, so there was suffering. Yet thousands left to join the armed forces, and even more migrated to cities to take defense jobs. These people were exposed to non-Indian society and returned with new insights. Following the war, they committed themselves to improve tribal government and to resist further intrusion by federal agencies, as well as to demand compensation for past wrongs.

The fourth section, "Today and Tomorrow," focuses on the 1950s and 1960s, when federal officials responded to Indian demands for less intrusion into their affairs, almost to the point of disaster. Congressmen legislated to "terminate" federal responsibility for Indian affairs and to "relocate" as many as possible in urban centers where they might be fully assimilated into non-Indian society. Both policies soon fell into disuse because they imposed readjustment at an impossible pace. Accordingly, in the 1960s federal officials took a more moderate posture. Most of them now stood ready to help in response to requests from the Indians themselves, but no longer gave unsolicited advice. The result of this posture, which offered "self-determination," was considerable improvement in housing and in economic development on reservations.

For all the good intentions of federal administrators in the 1960s, there remained widespread dissatisfaction. The inequities of centuries were not to be so rapidly overcome; Indian people could not prepare themselves in a few years to compete in the "dominant society." Non-Indians did not extend to them full civil rights. To resolve these problems, different types of Indian leaders emerged to act. One type, represented in Cato Valandra's interview, inspired progressive economic development among tribes. Another type, represented in the address of Lehman Brightman (a "militant" spokesman) spoke out to demand full civil rights and compensation for past abuses. Meanwhile, Indian people on reservations strove to recover the lost elements in their cultures—and began to cherish their "Indianness." They looked to a future of self-determination and self-realization unprecedented in Indian history since the arrival of European cultures.

Vermillion, South Dakota   J. H. C.
August 1971   H. T. H.

Contents

Things that guide the people

Noah White

An authority on the culture of the Winnebago tribe, Noah White lives at Prairie Island Indian Community, near Red Wing, Minnesota.

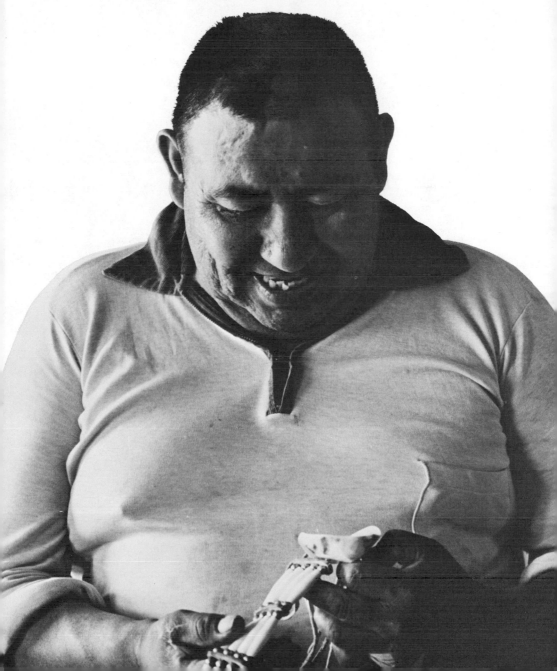

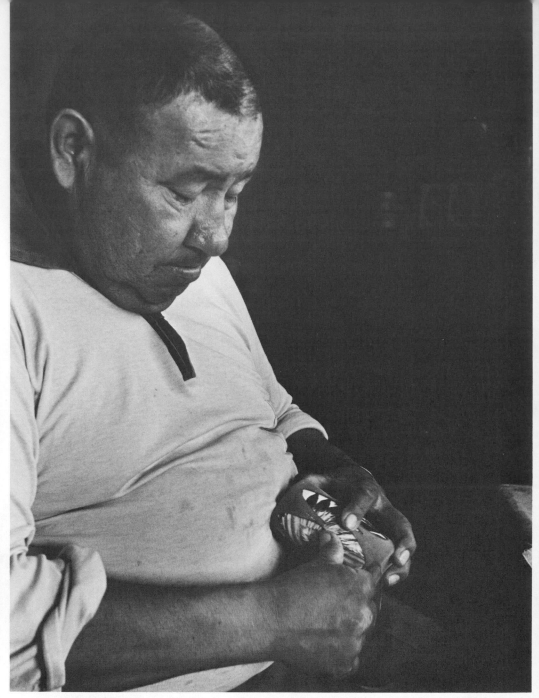

As a craftsman, Mr. White is known for his excellent heavy beadwork. The necklaces and other bead ornaments that he makes are either used by his family in ceremonial dancing or sold. He also makes Indian drums, ingenious in their use of twentieth-century materials. The hollow barrel is a tin can. An Indian scene of his own creation painted on paper decorates the outside; and after an Indian "pony bead" is placed inside for resonance, pieces of inner tube are laced tightly over the ends with leather.

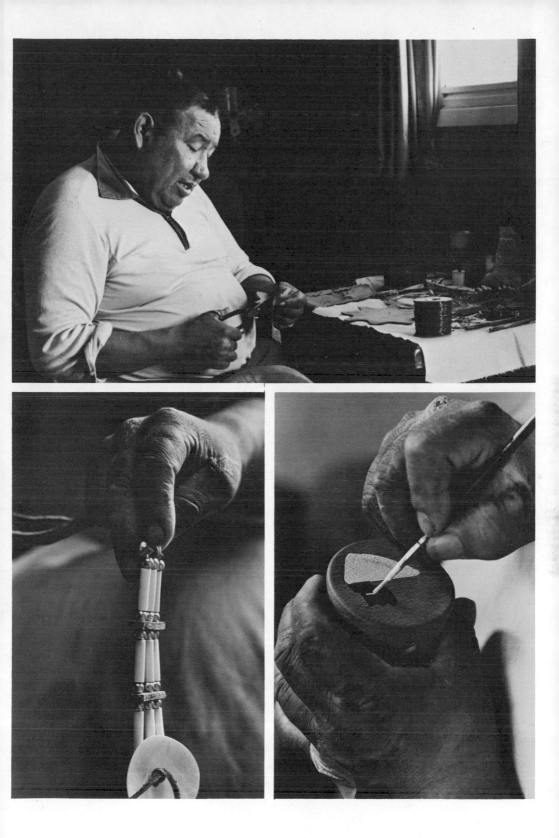

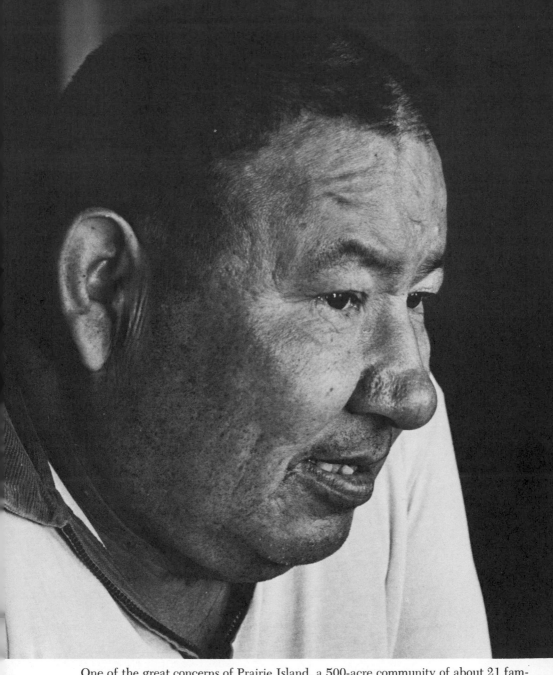

One of the great concerns of Prairie Island, a 500-acre community of about 21 families (approximately 80 residents) bordering on the Mississippi River, is a nuclear power plant now under construction on the adjacent land. When the reactors are fired up next year, hot refuse will pour into the river. Some tribal members predict the community will disappear within two or three years, despite power company official statements that the reactors are harmless. Mrs. White, her daughter Sandy, and her granddaughter hose down their auto (opposite, center). Sandy, 12, Ann, 17, and Noah, Jr., toss a frisbee in their yard (opposite, bottom).

To celebrate the completion of a Human Rights Commission-sponsored course in Indian culture taught by anthropologist Vern Halman of Hamline University to the teachers in nearby Red Wing High School, the Indians of Prairie Island held a dinner at their community center.

Mrs. White, well known for her Indian fry bread, helped prepare the dinner (below).

After the dinner, a powwow was held at Red Wing High School where Prairie Island community members and visiting Indian dancers performed traditional Plains Indian dances for the Red Wing townspeople. Noah White is regarded among Winnebagos as one of the most competent dancers.

Jonas Keeble

Sisseton Sioux

Sisseton Reservation, South Dakota
Interviewed by Herbert T. Hoover
August 27, 1969

———

Jonas Keeble was educated at Genoa Indian School, worked as a stone mason across South Dakota, and at retirement engaged in "craft work to pass away time." Mr. Keeble was eighty-three years old at the time of this interview.

———

The Story of the Creation of Man
Told by a Member of the Sisseton Sioux Tribe

JONAS KEEBLE Many, many seasons ago, Wakantanka, the Breath Giver, the Holy One, walked in the trees of the Paha Sapa, the Black Hills. The trees were cool and the music of the streams made him happy.

Over the high hard rock the Eagle soared on great wings. Deer looked at Wakantanka and their delicate feet were full of beauty and grace. Moose and Elk dipped their great heads into the water to pull the sweet lake grasses. The great Black Bears, afraid of nothing, padded toward the honey trees. Antelope stood deep in the meadow grasses.

But with all this beauty around him, Wakantanka was uneasy. He was happy and loved the Hills he had made, but there was no one he could love. No one who could return his love.

To all his creatures he had given something of himself: Strength to the Bear—Swiftness to the Hawk—Grace to the Deer—Perseverance to the Turtle—Majesty to the Eagle.

But there was something still in him that he must share—it was Love. And this was his greatest gift of all. This part of himself would make his work perfect. So he must take care of giving it.

11

Mother, the Earth, lay off toward the Rising Sun. She, too, stirred with life and stretched out her body trying to give birth to love. She crooned in her yearning:

My body is yours, Life Giver. You made me a
mother of many children. I nurse them. I
feed them. They grow and multiply everywhere.
But I see you are still lonesome, my Husband.
I have been faithful to you and have slept
with no other. But my children do not have
all of you in them. They are like me, and
hide in me. Now take my red flesh. Dig deep
in it. Tear it. I give it all to you. I
care not if afterwards I am called a Dead
Land. It is myself and all the love I can
give you.
When your son is born you will look at him
at first rising and at evening. You will
know he is your son. He will look like you.
He will turn his face to you and love you.

Mother, the Earth, sang her song day after day, and her love never grew less. The wind heard her words and carried them to the Holy Hills where Wakantanka listened, and he looked out over the prairies, wishing.

The wind knew the heaviness of his Heart and gently it spoke in the night to the Mother:

Mother, I will help you offer yourself, I
would never touch you, but I know there is no
other way to satisfy your prayer. In the
morning I will call my strong brother from
the south. He will bleach the grass that
covers you and tear it away from you. He
will lift it up like a cloud, and your body
will bleed. It will be red like the sun and
then you can say, 'Breath Giver, take this
part of me; from me make children like yourself and they will love you as I do.'
SleepingMother, are you ready for this hurt?

"Yes, Yes," the Mother sang. "Do it to me. And do not wait for the dawn. Call the south wind now and let him begin. I will sing with him. There will be no tears or pain. I am close to the Holy Hills and will always see how happy the Father is, and how loving are our children."

The south wind was not cruel. It worked gently and warmly. A new sound began to whisper in the valley of the hills. The Deer lifted their heads to catch a new scent. The Eagle whirled farther from his high home. Wakantanka turned his eyes here and there. All his creatures were silent.

Stars blazed at night, and a stillness came. The great red sun lifted itself to see what was new . . . and there on a high bare red hill stood upright a new thing.

Head thrown back, fingers and arms outstretched, red as the sun, swift as the deer, wise as the owl, loving as the Mother, stood Man, the Son of God, the one being who could say *A-te*, Father.

Ignace Garry

Coeur d'Alene

Coeur d'Alene Reservation, Idaho
Interviewed by Cornelius Byrne, S.J.
1956
Researched by Robert C. Carriker
July 1970

Ignace Garry, last chief of the Coeur d'Alene tribe, was nearly
seventy years old when he related the following story on creation
to a missionary Jesuit.

IGNACE GARRY   Years ago past, must be four or five hundred years or
more, at one time there was a flood over this land. This was on the Spokane
prairie. The water came higher and higher, and the [animal] people fled.
They fled to the place called Mount Spokane. They reached the top of the
mountain and there they stood. The people were terrified, and the water
kept rising closer and closer to them. They built out of whatever they could
find up on top of the mountain, tied them together, and built a large raft.
There they all got on the raft, and the mountain was flooded. The people
were very much afraid, they thought that they would never see land again,
that they were going to perish in the water. Oh, God, I can't remember that!

They were very afraid, and they talked among themselves and won-
dered what to do. So they told the loon—they had a hard time talking him
into it because he was also very afraid—they told him to dive down as far
as he could, and when you reach earth get some in your claws and bring
some back. When you come back to the surface, give the pieces of earth
to me. Although the loon—as you all know—is very long-winded, he is a
good diver [but] he didn't make it, he drowned. He didn't make it to the
bottom. They tried—after the loon came up and had not reached bottom
and died on his way up—they tried to talk all of the other animals into

14

going down. They tried to talk all of them into diving, all of the good divers that were known, the animals that were known for their diving abilities. They had almost given up, they sent out many, many animals that tried to dive down and couldn't make it down to the bottom, or even to the top of the mountain, the water was so high.

So they looked on their raft, and there was this tiny little animal sitting way on the back and keeping very quiet—the muskrat. So they told him, they said, "Come here, muskrat, we want you to dive. It is your turn now to dive down and try to get a handful of earth from the deep." The muskrat looked at them, and he says, "Not me! I am a poor little animal. I am pitiful. I am not capable of doing these things. If there was no way that the loon could do it or the others, I don't have a chance. They were all very good divers. The loon and all of the other animals were very good. I cannot do this, have pity on me and do not ask me. I am just a small little animal." However, the leader says, "No, I am asking you and you will do as I say."

I don't know how many times they had to coax him and coax him, and finally he said, "Oh, all right, I will. I'll do my best." So the little muskrat stood on the edge of the raft. He was very, very much afraid and he tried to dive in, and then he would pull back, try to dive in, and he finally went down. When he dove in, his heart was right in his mouth. He was so scared, he thought, "I will never return. Even if I reach the bottom, even if I don't come back, it's all right. At least I will get a handful of earth to bring back to the people." He dove, and it was very, very deep, a very deep dive, and he was able to reach earth, and he dug in his claws pieces of mud, and he started to come back up. He kicked with his leg to bring himself back up, but he lost consciousness. When he floated back up to the top of the water, only his back was visible.

The people pulled him out of the water and put him on the raft. They examined his paws, he had no earth. However, upon examining more closely they found that in his nails there were bits of mud, and from there, from his fingernails or whatever they were, they scraped the bits of earth and put it together. From this earth, little tiny bits of earth that they dug from the muskrat's claws, the head chief blew upon this earth, this little bit of mud. And it became larger. Every time he blew on it, it became larger and larger. He blew and he blew and he blew, and with each breath the earth became larger and larger and larger.

I don't know how many times he blew on this, and he turned around and commanded the fox. He told the fox, "You are to travel from one end of this earth to the other and come back and tell us how large this piece of earth is." So the fox started out on his journey, he ran as fast as he could; however, he was back in one day. The fox came back, he told the chief, "The land I have seen is quite large," he says, "I went from shore to shore and played on each shore." He was told by the chief, "No, some day there are going to be a lot of people on this earth. We must make it larger. We must make it now big enough to inhabit all of the people that will be here." So he kept blowing and blowing, and the earth kept becoming larger and larger.

After blowing many more times, they again commanded the fox to see how large the earth was from shore to shore. This time it took the fox one month. The fox returned. He said, "Boy, this is really a lot of ground," he says. "There is no way that the people of tomorrow are going to run out of soil." He was told by the head chief, "No, there are going to be millions and millions of people on this earth and to be back within one month, the earth is too small. We must make this earth large enough to take care of all of the people that will be here in the future. After all this is the earth [that] is not going to be really for us; it is to be for the people to come."

So they kept blowing and blowing larger and larger. So they told the fox to do this again, see how large this earth is. That was over a year and the fox had not returned, this must be a real, very large earth because the fox has not come back yet. So the earth became large enough for all of the people, for all of the future-coming people to inhabit. So there again it was the legends that built this earth. That is what is called North America today. It was built by the animal people. We here in the West, we who are sitting here wouldn't know each other today if it weren't so. Those, and there are people, millions and millions that we don't know who live in the East from where the sun rises. We just know people from here where the sun sets. I am not saying Noah was a liar, but I am not trying to add anything to Noah's story but the story is similar, it is close to the teachings of the way Noah put it out.

George Smith

Winnebago

Winnebago Reservation, Nebraska
Interviewed by Herbert T. Hoover
August 1970

Mr. Smith was eighty-six years old at the time of this interview.

GEORGE SMITH   I want to tell you about the happy hunting ground. When someone dies, they sit upon the earth four days before they go up on the way—go to the right or go to the left. They believe the way to hell means second death; that's their belief. Going to the right goes to heaven; that's their belief.

When I was a boy, I used to know one old man who talked for dead people, four nights. And they eat four nights. And on the fourth morning, this old man sang for them—sang for their souls—talking to dead souls, to the soul of the dead person. And he said, "I talk now. I'm going to tell the way you're going. On the fourth morning, you make your own family, your father, all stirred up. But that has got to be that way. Now, you're going to leave on the fourth morning. You leave all the good nuts and fruits to your family when you go. You're through with them." That is what he told the soul.

"Now you go on a trail to the west. You come to a wigwam. And you go in. And an old lady is sitting by the campfire. And you go sit down on the opposite side. Pretty soon she takes her wooden pan and puts some corn soup in there and gives it to you. You eat, just a little bit, and hand it back to her. And she'll say, 'Well, son, you done all right. Sometimes they eat them all up. But you leave some for me. You done all right.' And she sits down.

"When you go from here, there is a lot of places. How do you get through? There is a lot of thorn and patches. And black clouds come over. And she said, 'So you go over here on the trail to the west, looking for

17

two places. You come to a road. It severs. One goes to the right; one goes to the left. And there, there come to meet you your relations. And they take you to the wigwam, where the road passed on to the right and left of the wigwam. And you got to stay there four days. You're going to have your test. If you can't make it, you got to go to the left. If you make it, you go to the right.'

"The people living on the left side, they do nothing there during the day. But when night comes, after sundown, they'll commence being noisy —that's the noisy people. They're not the good people. But the others, they are all right. They got their own minds, and they are happy all the time."

And this old man talking, told to him what he was going to go through. Now he says, "I'm going to sing for you. And you must sing that when you get closer—closer to the place. And there your relations will say, 'That's him.' Or 'That's her.' They heard you at the wigwam at the fork." And this old man sang for his soul, a song.

And now with the soul singing, when it gets near, they come to meet him. The relations, they come, and they take him to that wigwam, situated near the fork of the trail, where one road goes to the right, and one goes to the left. He goes in there, and they tell him, "You have to have your test— for four days and four nights, right here. You got to stay in here." That's what they tell him. So he goes in there and sits down. He waits. And they have a blanket on him.

And on the path that goes on the right, he could hear some talking, laughing. But on the path on the left side, he never heard anybody up there. It was as quiet as could be. That's where the bad people are. In the evening, he was sitting there, in the wigwam. It was sundown. And pretty soon he hears someone up in that camp, making noises. Pretty soon there are women laughing, and talking—they get noisy in the camp, talking and laughing. And he sat there. He took his blanket and covered his head. Pretty soon he heard a drum coming on this left side. And they're singing.

They come in. They go around the wigwam outside. They commence dancing and singing. He sat there. And pretty soon some women laughed and said, "What's the sense of the blanket?" And they tried to pull this blanket. "Come talk to me. You're nice-looking. Look at me a while, and see what kind of looking woman I am." They just bothered him all night. And that was the test, see.

But he stuck to it. Of course, he wanted to see them—what they looked like. A young man—young women talking to him. He said then, "Why didn't they go home to their camp?" It was sunup—sun began to come up. It was quiet all at once. No more noise. He did that four nights. If he didn't look at them by sunrise, those people, his relations come in—come get him. He made it. He made this test. They took him home to their camp. He sees all his relations there. Most of them at the camp are good people. Now, that's the story of how he gets to the happy hunting ground.

George Smith

Winnebago

Winnebago Reservation, Nebraska
Interviewed by Herbert T. Hoover
August 1970

Mr. Smith was eighty-six years old at the time of this interview.

GEORGE SMITH Indians were camping during the summer. They prayed to God. And in the fall they moved to a winter camp where there were good hunting grounds. That was my people. One man went by the name of Lone Wolf. He's a smart man, a good hunter, goes on the warpath always. His wife, she's younger than him; she's pretty. They were going to move to winter camp and get ready. And he sent the camp caller out to tell the people to get ready in four days. "After four days we are going to move," the chief said. So Lone Wolf told his wife. He said, "I'll go. I'll get some fresh meat. I have to go quite a ways."

He hated dogs. Everybody at camp knows that he hated dogs. Sometimes a dog come in the wigwam door, stick his nose in there, and he takes his knife and cut the dog's nose off. Things like that. And he's got a little boy and a little girl who can't have little pups. When he comes home he sees that little pup there. He just took that pup and hit on a tree, and threw it outside. He just hated dogs. All the dogs know him, too.

Lone Wolf went hunting, and he got sick out there and laid down. He had some kind of fever over there. When they have that fever, they're out of their heads. He had that when he was out hunting, and he didn't come back. I don't know how long he laid out there. Finally he came to. He tried to hunt, but saw he was too weak. So he came home with the use of a stick. When he got to his camp, the camp was empty. Nobody was there. They already moved and left him. So he picked up some of what they used for wigwams, and he made a little round hut for himself and stayed there all night. The next day he went out and he found some dry meat up on a tree that they left for him—his people left dried meat—deer meat. He brought this to his little wigwam and put it on to cook. He ate that meat, and he felt better.

The camp was quiet, nothing there. After dark he was sitting there by the campfire, in the round hut, you know, with a smoke hole up there. He was sitting there and watching it. And from way off somewhere, he heard a dog howling. Pretty soon, a pup, that the people left, barked. He listened. Lone Wolf listened. Pretty soon that old dog came in that door. He had few hairs on him; he was an old dog. He had a little pup. They both come in and sat across on the other side of the campfire. They sat down, and he said, "You shut up." They try to touch his heart. He hated dogs. But they pity him. And pretty soon he got his meat down, he cut it up and he fed them. He put the soup down for them, and they ate.

The next morning he talked with them, and he fed them. He had some corn, dry corn, that he ate himself. He carried that with him all the time. After sunrise he started out. Lone Wolf, he took that little pup and threw him on his back. The old dog followed behind.

At evening he made a campfire. And the old dog was barking at a little stump. Lone Wolf finally went over there to look. There was a bear, the size of a big tree stump. That was why he was barking. So Lone Wolf stabbed him with a wooden knife, stuck the knife in him. He killed that bear, and he cut it open some way, and he cut some meat and cooked it. He cooked some meat for himself and the dogs.

Lone Wolf traveled four days. Every evening, the old dog would find something to eat, fresh meat. When he got to the camp, everybody came out of the camp and said, "Hello, hello. Lone Wolf came back—he came back." Everybody came out of their wigwams and looked at him. He had a little dog on his back. They all knew that he hated dogs. And he asked where his folks were, and they took him to his wife and two children. He took the little dog and gave it to his kids. His mother came, and his father came; they were glad to see him.

And one day a warpath came, and they had a battle. The other tribe was Sioux Indians, from up north. Close to evening they quit. Those Sioux quit, all of them pulled out. So Lone Wolf came back, but his wife didn't come back. They captured his wife. He had a pretty woman, and they took her. They took her, so he just had him and two children left.

He said, "Tomorrow, I'm going after my wife. I'll track them down. I'm going to get my wife." Next morning, his mother fixed some mocassins for him. He took a lot of dry corn, and he started out—had a bow and arrow and knife. That evening he stopped by the tent where that war party slept. At the campfire, on the ashes, he saw some hair; his wife did that. He knew that was his wife's hair. He went after her. Finally he got there, to a ridge. There was brush all over. Down on the other side was a little stream. Nothing but plains from there on, just plains. A lot of horses all over— Sioux Indians' horses. He thought he'd go down to the spring. He saw the women coming down by the creek to get water there. He thought he'd go sit over there—and his wife would come. So he went over there and sat down and waited. He didn't know about his wife, that they made her marry the chief's son. He didn't know she was married to that young man.

And while he was sitting there his wife came after water and he called her by her name. He said, "Leave that bucket there. Let's go right now. Let's go home." She was crying, lonesome. And the woman said, "Just wait for me. Just wait for me. I'll take this water and I'll come back, and then we'll go." She went. But she went back to her husband and she told him. "There's a man down at the spring, from some other tribe," she said to her husband. She didn't want to go home to him, see. And so a brave went out there and they caught him. They caught him sitting there. They tied him up. He was going to die. They put four stakes in the ground, and then they lay him there and tied rawhide on his wrists. Then the next morning, they would go and kill him.

Everybody was going to ride their horses, to run right over him. That's the way they were going to kill him. They were coming, you know, on a bunch of horses; and when they got close he just wiggled around as much as he could and kept moving. The horses stepped over him. When he would move around, they never stepped on him. He just kept moving around. The horses knew it was a human, they wouldn't step on him. And they all were gone. No one looked back. They just went on home, and left him for dead—all smashed up, they think.

But it didn't kill him. So he lay there. He just thought somehow if he could get loose he would go home. He tried to work himself loose. After dark, somewhere far away, at the edge of the camp, he heard dogs howling. He knew that was his dog. But if he would only come closer, that dog. He started to yell. The dog came and started chewing on that rawhide. He cut his master loose. After they got so far, they ate. That old dog would kill something. They ate, and they got home to where his people looked after him.

Now, these people captured his wife back, but they put her in the castaway; as long as she lived they put her on the edge of the camp. She ate whatever she could get. She was not one of the tribe anymore, because of what she had done to this husband. Her mother goes over there, and takes her something to eat. The mother's love is next to God's love. But Lone Wolf—it was a big hurt to him. They want to know what he's going to do to her—kill her or whatever. Whatever he did, it would be all right. So they brought her over to Lone Wolf's wigwam. She came, and she sat down. They said, "Lone Wolf, come, take this knife, and stick her and kill her." They all said that. But he said to her, "Woman I forgive you. For what you have done to me, I forgive you. Now get out of here. Go back to your wigwam." That's what he told her. He forgave her. He had learned, with his dog, to love and forgive. And he forgave her.

Mitch Michael

Coeur d'Alene

Coeur d'Alene Reservation, Idaho
Interviewed and Researched by
Thomas Connolly, S.J., and Robert C. Carriker
July 1970

This Coeur d'Alene, past sixty years old, lives on the tribal reservation.

Why There are So Many Mosquitoes on the Kalispel Reservation

MITCH MICHAEL   That Mosquito and his grandmother, they had one tipi; they lived in one. They must have been alone. I don't know how it begins, but they were together and his grandmother was killed. I don't know by what, but anyhow she was killed. Well, that's when Mosquito got to look to get revenge for his grandmother, so he came down on the boat and go down the first camp, or it would be village. Well, he took his canoe down there and then he'd go in, go to the camp. Well, he had a spear and he chased the kids and everybody around and everybody was scared of him. Well, it got to be a monster.

So they finally got into the long house and they were all scared of him, and then they feed him where he can eat it. When he was going on his canoe, and when he got to the opening to the camp, then they hollered at him, "Come on, Mosquito, we're going to have something to eat. We got wheat, grain, soup, and all that." And he says he doesn't eat that. He doesn't like that. Finally one of them hollered, he says, "We got blood, a bowl of blood, warm." And he says, "Well, that's the one I'd like," and then he went to the camp. He got to the camp and inside, and they had a bowl of blood. Well, he drink that all out and got no more. Then they kicked his bowl and broke it and throwed it away and then he was just scaring everybody. They were all afraid of him. So he went back on his canoe, and he went down to another camp, where they asked him to eat and the same thing and no, he refused and nothing but blood. Well, that's the one he goes for. Well, the second or third camp where he got so big, eat too much, drink too much blood, so then he went in there, and after he got out of there and they didn't know how they could get rid of him.

And every time, before he gets to the next camp, they're wondering how they kill him or get rid of him. So one of the men says, well that's easy. He says, "When he gets here and while he is eating, we will push his canoe out in the river, where he will have to swim for his canoe to get it back and while he's swimming, throw a pine needle on the water, it will be going downstream." He says, "That will kill him."

And so on the next camp he done the same thing, and he wanted, got his meal, and he went down, after he got through with his bucket and then he starts killing a lot of them before he gets. They told him that your boat is gone, they pushed it. Oh, then he was mad then when he got there, and he seen his boat way out and it was going, and he runned down below and that's when he swimmed. That's when they put these pine needles on the water and they all float down and one of the needles stuck his belly, that's when he started flying and this must have been, well, it must have been in Kalispel [Reservation] around in there. That's where he went up in the cottonwood tree He was buzzing around in there, and I think it was Coyote that told him, "That's all, that's where you are going to stay, in those trees, and when the sun comes and when the spring comes, there will be lots of mosquitoes." That's all that I know about that.

Variations of this legend by certain Kalispel and Spokane Indians name the blood-drinking offender as an outlaw or monster, with the pine-needle bursting by the Kalispel tribesmen transforming him into a mosquito that could continue to suck blood, but never kill.

Celina Goolsby

Coeur d'Alene

Spokane, Washington
Interviewed by Robert C. Carriker
July 1970

Celina Goolsby, a Coeur d'Alene, is the daughter of Ignace
Garry, last chief of her tribe. In her middle fifties during this
interview, Mrs. Goolsby offers here a family story involving the
Coyote, central figure in most Interior Salish tribe legends.

CELINA GOOLSBY   Okay. So the Coyote was walking and all of a sudden
he heard a bunch of kids screaming and crying and everything, and he went
over there and he says, "What's your matter? What's your matter? How
come you are screaming? You are crying!" They said, "Oh, Coyote, Coyote,
there's a big monster over there, a people-eater, and he's eating up all the
little kids." And the Coyote says, "I'll just put his lights out!" So he sneaked
over and he saw this great big people-eater who had been eating kids, and
he was fat, fat, fat, just laying there.

So the Coyote gathered up a bunch of rocks, nice little round rocks,
and he wrapped them in skins and he tied them around his ankles and he
tied them around his wrists, and he got a little ways from the ogre and he
started dancing and he started singing. And you could hear the sounds
of the rocks, you know, making the beautiful noise, you know. And the
Coyote would look; and he would look to the side to see if the ogre would
look, and he would just keep dancing and singing, and he'd dance, dance,
dance.

After a while, the ogre says, "Coyote! Coyote! Come here!" The Coyote
wouldn't pay any attention; he just kept singing. Meantime, there is this
wonderful sound. "Coyote, Coyote, please, Coyote, come here." "Oh, all
right then." So the Coyote went over to the ogre and the ogre says, "What
is that sound? That wonderful sound is in your legs." The Coyote says, "Oh,

that's in my bones, hear it?" And you could hear the sound. "Is there any way that you can help me so that I can do that?" "No, that's my bones. My bones are all broken, and when I dance they rattle." So he kept dancing and he'd dance around.

And so the ogre asked him, he said, "Could you make me like that, so that I'd be able to dance and make that sound?" The Coyote says, "Oh, no, no, no. That'd be too hard on you. It hurts! You've got to be really strong and you've got to have courage," he says. "Anything like this, the pain would be too much for you. You just wouldn't live through it. It takes a man like me." And the Coyote would dance, dance, dance, and the ogre begged and begged and begged.

He says, "Well, all right, we'll try it. You put your legs out." So the ogre put his legs out, and the Coyote come up with a big rock and smashed one leg. "Ow, oww, oww, ohh, that hurts, that hurts, that hurts!" And he smashed down on the other leg, and the ogre was screaming in agony and moaning and groaning. Smashed his arms so that he'd be able to get this sound in his arms, and the ogre says, "Now Coyote, what do I do?" And the Coyote says, "You fool! You'll never eat children again, you'll never be able to eat them again."

And that's the end of the story.

Paul Picotte

Yankton Sioux

Lake Andes, South Dakota
Interviewed by Joseph H. Cash
June 1968

Paul Picotte is regarded by Indians as the chief authority on tribal history among the Yanktons. A graduate of Haskell Institute, he is a descendant of the famed fur trader and Indian agent, Andrew Drips. Mr. Picotte was eighty-eight years old at the time of this interview.

PAUL PICOTTE   The last burial I saw on a scaffold was in 1888 right down at Greenwood. And the fellow—they called him Hiram Smith—he was buried on a scaffold there with a buffalo robe tied around him. He was all bones, and one my schoolmates went over there and drug [dragged] the robes right off of that corpse right up on that scaffold.

They finally took the remains down, what was left of it. and I don't know how many years it'd been buried there, but they took it up to one of the cemeteries and buried it up there. They even used to bury them in trees. But after they took this old fellow's bones down there in Greenwood. that scaffolding stuff just disappeared.

Father Vine Deloria

Sioux

Vermillion, South Dakota
Interviewed by Herbert T. Hoover
November 30, 1970

Father Deloria enjoys great respect among both Indians and
non-Indians across the Middle West as a clergyman and moral
leader. An Episcopal priest for several decades, he was in his
sixties and rector of St. Paul's Episcopal Church at
Vermillion, when interviewed.

FATHER DELORIA The Yanktons had six or seven chiefs, each of maybe
seven or eight hundred people. My grandfather was Chief of the White
Swan Yankton. That was one of the smallest ones, about six hundred I
guess. When he died, all the Yanktons chose my father, because Struck-by-
the-Ree was also gone—the top chief of all the Yanktons. Imagine this—he
was chosen chief at the age of eighteen. My, people matured in those
days . . . .

I was in Washington attending the college of preachers as a fellow
. . . and a woman called, and she said, "My mother wants me to take you
home . . . because she wants to show you something." So I went out there.
Mrs. Lightfoot, her name was, she brought out an old diary—worn—that
belonged to her father. He was a missionary to the Poncas, right across the
river from the Yanktons. And he said in there, "Today I rode over in a boat
to see the installation of the new young chief of all the Yanktons, Philip
Deloria, age eighteen."

He wasn't chief very long . . . . He had his hair cut, and got all cleaned
up, and went to . . . a little college in Platsmouth, Nebraska. I don't know
what the name of the college was. It is no longer there. He and Felix Bruno,
another Yankton, went there. Then they came back. He hadn't gone into the
ministry yet, but they made him kind of a lay-reader. They made those men
take charge of a congregation. So he did.

That's where this remarkable organization started called the Brotherhood of Christian Unity. When my father was nineteen, he had joined and
had gone to school, and he had come back summers—as had Felix Bruno
and David Tateopa. Those three—all Yanktons—got to talking. And they
said the country is going to be overrun by whites. Our people shouldn't be
trying to run and lead the "old life." They ought to settle and learn how
to make a living on the land. The Government is willing to give them
equipment. And so let's encourage our people along that line.

Also, they were talking about ecumenical movement. These three
young kids—my father was nineteen, Felix Bruno was twenty, David Tateopa, twenty-one. My father was headed for the ministry. Yet, they discussed the fact that the many Yanktons who joined the Christian church
were either Romans or Episcopalians, Congregationalists, or Presbyterians.
They noted that in those days—that's ninety-seven years ago—it was causing
the people to become aloof from one another. And they said, "Let's have a
Sioux united movement." They were talking about the Brotherhood. In
those days there was a great deal made of the idea of whatever each
church taught, it was the only way to Heaven . . . . But these three young
men said, "Let's make an attempt to maintain Dakota unity. Our Sioux is
a hard enough guy to unite. Christianity is a wonderful religion, but with
that attitude, somebody is wrong. They can't all be right. And they won't
admit that the others might have something—'Oh, be careful of the Presbyterians, be careful of the Romans, be careful of the Congregationalists, be
careful of the Episcopalians, and so on.' That's making even relatives aloof
—that feature in the life of American Indian religion. Let's just live with
God day after day, as part of life."

In other words, they were three-dimensional people. Here is the
physical, the intellectual, and the spiritual. So they weren't lopsided guys.
I can tell you that. They weren't two-dimensional . . . . There was a length
and a breadth and a height to their lives. No wonder Columbus admired
Indians, as did other explorers, and George Catlin, who said such wonderful
things. And so it was as they started the Brotherhood.

It is still going. It's very weak right now, but in three years it will
have its first centennial . . . . It was to help the people settle down. Too, it
was more of a social thing. They are interested in anything that is good for
the people; they would go after broken families. You see, they lack economic resources. These days, it seems like you have to have money to get
anything done. It shouldn't be so, but it is. That's why the impact is no
longer what it used to be.

They were numbered about one thousand at one time. That's a lot
of Indians for brotherhood. These four churches used to look at them as
outlaws, counterfeits . . . . My father was BCU [Brotherhood of Christian
Unity]. He was a priest in the Episcopal Church, and other Indian priests
said he was a counterfeit, practicing two religions. But we were just trying

to live three-dimensional lives like our ancestors. Younger people, they said, all joined different churches. So let's go ahead and carry on in those churches. But let's maintain this unity among ourselves. Another thing I like about this . . . as long as you talk about Jesus, I can dig it.

Noah White

Winnebago

Prairie Island Indian Community, Minnesota
Interviewed by Herbert T. Hoover
June 25, 1970

Mr. White, the only member of the Winnebago tribe at Prairie
Island, is a skilled craftsman, an excellent dancer, and a leader
in the Native American Church. He was fifty-three years old at
the time of this interview.

HERBERT HOOVER   You are a member of the Native American Church.
. . . Have you belonged to it for a long time?

NOAH WHITE   Well, from just prior to when I went into the service
[during World War II]. I went there on my own accord. It's just like going
to any other church. I mean, you like a certain denomination, and that's
more or less where you want to put your faith and everything towards
God. And I thought the Native American Church was the way I wanted
to believe. To my way of thinking, it's one of the most humble churches in
the world today, because actually there aren't too many chapters that have
a church of their own. They go to worship in different peoples' homes; they
sit on the floor, and instead of staying an hour or two hours in the church,
they worship all night from dusk until dawn—they sit there and worship all
night long. The songs are similar to the hymns that you have in church.
The prayers—there isn't any prayer that's memorized—all come from within
the person, whatever you want to speak to God—your troubles, and your
tribulations, and your trials—whatever it may be. You turn them over to
the Father, Son, and the Holy Ghost. It's a humble way of worship. Most
Indians that belong to it try to live that way in their everyday lives. It
teaches you to try to have good fellowship with everybody—everyone that
you meet—and to try to help your fellow brothers. It more or less runs along

the lines of a common-prayer meeting. That's what it is. The ones that sponsor it, I imagine, could use the money that they spent for that for personal reasons. But they figure that whatever is spent towards God is never lost. They will get it back in one form or another.

Q   I gather that when you get together to worship, you start out with a certain ritual?

A   Yes, we have leaders that conduct these services. After everybody is seated at the home where the prayer service is held, the leader gets up and tells the people who the sponsor of the prayer service is, what his name is, and why they are having the prayer meeting. Then he calls upon the sponsor to get up and explain to the people why they are having the meeting.

So he [the sponsor] repeats what the leader has already said, but he more or less tells it in his own words. He greets them all first, and then he goes on to explain to them why they are having the prayer meeting, and he asks all the people for their help in prayers. And if there is someone sick, they offer special prayers for the healing of the sick, and then for the people that are in mourning who have lost a loved one. They ask special prayers for them to help them out in their daily lives. And during these trying times, when we are having conflicts here and there, for all of the boys that have volunteered into the armed services, they offer special services for them, too. So that maybe some day, if the good Lord sees fit, they would come home in good health and good spirit and take up their lives where they left off. And then they have the birthday meeting, and some other meetings which are happier occasions. That more or less covers just about all the meetings.

He [the leader] explains the purpose of each meeting to the people that have arrived from various places, and some people travel two or three hundred miles just to attend the prayer meetings, and then go back home and are back to work on a Monday morning. I mean, that's how much they believe in their church and in the Lord. But all that hardship, between getting there and getting back, doesn't mean too much to them. They think that at one time or another, they are going to be rewarded for all of that— not in this world, but in the life hereafter.

After that, the leader offers a prayer, and then they throw cedar in the ashes that the fireman brings in. They throw cedar in there, and then they smoke peyote that they use for a sacrament [on the ashes]. Then they smoke the drum, and the gourd, and the staff—whatever they are going to use in there. They have the Bible there; and they smoke that.

They set all those down, and then the fireman comes around, and he hands the sacrament to each one, starting with the leader. Some places he goes to the right, where the drum people sit, and then he goes to the left, where the cedar-man sits, and then from there he goes clockwise all the way around. After they eat the sacrament, they can start singing, and they can pray whenever they want and help each other out singing.

It's a real worship, where you are singing praises to the Lord just like you do in church. They start the staff, and the gourd, and the drum out. The leader sings first. Sometimes the drummer sings next, and at other meetings, the cedar-man. They just start from the leader and it goes clockwise. Each sings four songs, until it goes all the way around. In some places they stop right at midnight and they have a man pray, and they have a man talk about the scripture in the Bible. Most of the people that talk about it [the scripture] don't look in the Bible to see what they are going to preach about. They take a scripture out of the Bible [from memory] to fit the reason for the prayer meeting. Like if somebody is sick, they will talk about scripture in the Bible pertaining to somebody that was healed in the days when Jesus was around, and what He did to heal sickness; they give a sermon on that. It's all done in their own words. They more or less tear down the verses, word for word, and interpret each word, and then put it back together in sentence form.

After they get through with this, they stop at midnight, and the same thing starts off again. They pass out the peyote sacrament. Then they start out the singing again, and it goes around until about three o'clock, and then they do the same thing again. It's repeated, but they call on different ones to get up and pray; and then they call on different ones to get up and talk. They pick at random so when anybody attends these meetings, he's got to be able to get up if he is called on to pray and offer his prayer. Or if he is called on to give a little sermon, he's got to be able to get up and give a little sermon pertaining to the prayer meeting.

Then, about daylight, the staff and all the instruments get back to the leader again, and the same thing is done. But before they finish, they leave a little opening if anybody wants to get up and give a little talk. People can talk as long as they want to. They usually say that two people can get up and talk, but sometimes as many as four or five get up and just offer a little gratitude, thanking the people [responsible] for all the expenses they went through. After that, the leader sings four songs to end the prayer services. And after he sings these four songs, then they all stand up and offer a word of prayer, each one in his own manner. Sometimes they get members of four or five different tribes there, and they all are offering their prayers in their own languages. And with that, the meeting is over.

They put all the implements away, and then they visit around. They usually quit around six or seven o'clock in the morning, and then about nine o'clock the womenfolk have sandwiches, coffee, and rolls, and they have breakfast. After that, they visit around again, as the womenfolk are busy cooking up dinner, and they have dinner. And after that they go on their way home. That's about the extent of the prayer meeting.

Q   Where do you go to attend prayer meetings?

A   Well, I went a few times in Minneapolis, and then a few times

down in Winnebago, Nebraska. Once in a while, I go over into Wisconsin
. . . . Over in Wisconsin they send a letter, or they call up in the cities
[Minneapolis and St. Paul], and some of the members from the cities come
down and let us know. They have ways and means of notifying people.

Q   Where in Wisconsin do they have meetings?

A   Well, they have a regular church in Wisconsin along Old Highway 12 . . . . You see, at the church at Wisconsin Dells they have a bulle-
tin board where you reserve certain weekends for meetings . . . . And some
hold the services in their own homes.

Q   Where in Nebraska do you meet?

A   Well, more or less in the private homes.

Q   Is there a regular church in Minneapolis or St. Paul?

A   No. See, the chapter in Minnesota does not have a church at all.
They just meet at peoples' homes.

Q   Does each state have a chapter? Or is the church divided according to tribal groups?

A   No, they have to have a charter in the state capital, wherever
these chapters are located. Like in Wisconsin, they have a state chapter;
there is only one for the whole state of Wisconsin. But they have different
groups branching out from the state chapter. And each group has one member on the state board. There is a regular committee, a chairman, a vice-
chairman, a treasurer, a secretary, and a delegate-at-large. And then they
have custodians. Some places they are really organized. Like in South
Dakota, they have a regular ordained minister in their chapter . . . .

Q   Is the leader of the service simply somebody from the community
that offers to lead?

A   Well, the one that is sponsoring the prayer meeting selects the
leader. Just about all the older men are more or less qualified to conduct
the meeting. They know the laws that they have to run the meeting.

Q   You have mentioned peyote in relation to sacrament . . . . Is there
any special, important point in the service when you eat peyote?

A   The only time that you eat it is when you go into these prayer
meetings, and the leader offers a prayer to bless the peyote so that it will
help you to be more conscious. You are supposed to try to put your mind
more on the subject of worshipping. It's just like when you go to church and
you take Holy Communion. You have the wine there, and you have the
bread, and that probably pertains to the same thing that the peyote does.
They use it as a sacrament . . . .

Q   It there anything else about the Native American Church that
you would like to say?

A   Well, there isn't much more that I can say about it, outside of that
if anyone is really interested in learning about it, the best way—and the
quickest way—to learn is to attend the meetings and actually take part. You
hear in the news media and a lot of things are written about peyote that

most of the members disagree with; and it's written by people that actually haven't taken part in a prayer meeting.

Q   Well, how does a fellow like me get a chance to take part in a prayer meeting?

A   Wherever you hear of a meeting, get in contact with the officers in your own area . . . . They would be more than willing to have you come in and attend a meeting.

Sterling Snake

Winnebago

Winnebago Reservation, Nebraska
Interviewed by Herbert T. Hoover
July 29, 1970

———

Mr. Snake was one of the younger members of the Winnebago
tribal council when interviewed. He was thirty-eight years old at
the time.

———

STERLING SNAKE   When I was a baby my mother took me in and got
me baptized in the Dutch Reformed Church, being as she went to school
under the Dutch Reformed Church. And after I was older, she took me off
to a school in South Dakota, which is run by the Catholic Church. And after
I was there a year, when I was to go back to second grade, I told my mother
I wasn't baptized in the Catholic Church. I couldn't return to school, I said.
You have to be baptized in town. And I was also baptized in the Native
American Church. So naturally I'm baptized in three different religions. But,
on all of the Indian reservations we have this same thing, where all these
different denominations come to the reservation, like the missionaries. In
fact, through my research and stuff, I found out that even before the Bureau
was the head of the job on handling of the reservation, the churches were
given different reservations, you know. Before the Bureau took over, the
Government was sending these churches money, and stuff like this, to set up
schools for the Indians on different reservations. You might say the churches
were in the Indian business a long time before—before the Bureau was.

HERBERT HOOVER   I gather the Dutch Reformed Church has been the
biggest force here?

A   Well, in the earlier part of the 1800s to the earlier 1900s the
Catholic Church was pretty strong in this area, but since then the Dutch
Reformed Church has built up a lot of power.

Q How frequently do you have meetings in the Native American Church here?

A Well, the Native American Church usually has a meeting about every weekend. They usually have them on Saturday nights, and they run all night, and through Sunday.

Q Do you have a regular church building here?

A No, we hold them in the homes of different people that are sponsoring the meetings. [Sometimes] somebody sets up a tipi to have what they call a tipi meeting.

Q About how many members are there in the Winnebago area?

A I never did an actual count on how many members there are . . . . I would say there must be around . . . one hundred of them.

Q That's on the Winnebago Reservation?

A Right.

Q There are quite a few Omahas too?

A Well, I was reading where . . . about ninety percent of the Omahas belong to the Native American Church. That's where the national headquarters is.

Q I wonder if you would describe the nature of the all night meetings that you have?

A Well, we call them prayer meetings. They are given for different things—maybe to baptize a child, or some person has a birthday, or some person is sick . . . . Maybe somebody is given the first communion or somebody that has been sick has gotten well, . . . and they give a thanksgiving. Usually they run all night. What they do is, they go in, and at the meetings they have what they call a road man or a guy that runs the meetings. And with him are three assistants. One is a "bear chief." He does all the work that is necessary that night, in these prayer meetings. One is what they call a cedar tree. And one is what they call a drum tree. He accepts all of the drums and other things they use in the service. The meeting usually opens with the leader saying a prayer, giving the reason of the meeting. And then they start singing. When they sing their hymns, you might say [it is] in prayer . . . . The Indians sing . . . when the singing starts you have one man . . . [who] does the singing and then he has a guy drumming for him. And this guy helps him sing. And usually they sing four songs. Each man sings four songs, and they pass the instruments around to the next two people, who also sing four songs. When they get all around the tipi or all around the Indians in the prayer meeting, at twelve o'clock they make another start. They bring in water and bless it and pass water around . . . and have another prayer. And then they usually have somebody get up and talk, tell a Bible story, or talk on the subject of the meeting . . . . And then after this is done he starts singing, until three o'clock, when they make another stop and the leader asks somebody else to pray, and somebody else to get up and talk. Then they start singing again, and they usually sing 'til sunrise. And then they have their services at sunrise . . . . In the morning they have a little different type of service than the other ones. They bring in corn and meat and fruit as a sacrament at breakfast . . . . They stop their singing, and the leader gets up and prays again, and they ask somebody else to get up and talk again. And then they have this ceremonial breakfast. After the breakfast gets done, the leader will sit down and sing four more songs and then he closes the meeting. This is usually done about seven o'clock or eight o'clock in the morning, and then the rest of the day is spent visiting or talking about what happened the night before.

Q   Is the Bible a central part of this?

A   Yes, the Bible is the central part.

Q   So this is a Christian ceremony?

A   Right.

Q   Why do you think this came along to replace the other denominations?

A   Well, in my way of thinking it's the last thing of the Indian that is Indians'. And it's something they want to hang on to. I have said many a time in the prayer meeting, you know, this is something that God gives to the Indians . . . . It's the last thing Indian that the Indian has, and he wants to keep it.

Q   I gather, too, that the order of worship gives opportunity for individual expression.

A   Yes, we don't have any prayer books, or any hymnals, or anything, you know; it all comes from the heart.

Q   You offer sacrament?

A   Well, in these meetings, there is peyote. This is a small cactus you get down in Texas and New Mexico; that is about the only place it comes from, and this is what they use for sacraments there. They use this during the night; they also make tea out of it. They grind it up and make sort of a gravy out of it and eat it.

Q   They offer that usually one time in the night?

A   No, this is set by the leader, and any time anybody wants some of it they ask for it.

Q   How about outsiders? Do you allow them to come in?

A   Well, previously, about ten, even up to five years ago, we of the Native American Church allowed visitors into the meeting—allowed non-Indians to participate in the meeting—even the sacramental supper. Lately the "hippie movement," you know, and all these other movements, are moving in and using peyote not as a sacrament but as they might use pot, or something like this. This has brought on stricter laws . . . . Through the efforts of the president of the Native American Church, and other leaders of the Native American Church, they have got exempted from these laws. Native American Church members, they can use this peyote, and they can get it through the mail.

Q How would you respond to a fellow like me, who belongs to another Christian church, who comes to attend your meeting?

A Well, I will tell you about a thing that happened recently . . . . [A non-Indian] was quite interested in Indian ways. We had one fellow take him to our meeting. He went to see what it was like, and he ate peyote. And the next morning, it just happened that the national president was sitting in on this meeting. Next morning the president got up and told him that he was jeopardizing the Indians' use of peyote by coming in and taking part in the meeting, observing the church . . . . He said he realized he wasn't going to hurt anything, but he was still jeopardizing the Indians' use of peyote.

Q Then you prefer that other people not come in.

A Right.

John Cummins

Crow

Crow Agency, Montana
Interviewed by Stuart Connor
October 1970

Mr. Cummins is a former Crow tribal chairman and one of the more experienced Sun Dancers of the Crow. He was probably in his seventies at the time of this interview.

STUART CONNOR How many Sun Dances have there been since the Crows adopted their current Sun Dance?

JOHN CUMMINS Around fifty, I think. The Sun Dance that the Crows have originated with the Shoshones in Wyoming brought over. The Crows had their own Sun Dance. It's something similar to this; you might say it's the same thing. Where they fast in there for three days and three nights. And the Sun Dance is very sacred.

Q How many Sun Dances have you danced in?

A Forty-three. I've been in forty-three of them.

Q Can you tell me about the physical part of the Sun Dance—the cutting of the trees, the building of the lodge, and the various songs and dances that go on through the whole thing?

A The belief of the Indian is that everything on the earth that is created was created by one person. Now you take the trees and the grass and the sagebrush and anything that grows and has a root and that grows on the ground was made or created by this one person which has a meaning of life, and that's the root of the Indian religion. And the white people say nature, see. The tree represents life. The leaves represent life. I mean that they cure certain diseases, certain sicknesses. And when a man uses these things, he believes in this creator. He believes that these things could be done by believing. The white man says faith and hope. The Sun Dance is the same way.

When you go into a Sun Dance, you go out and pray with the center pole, center post; it's a forked post. I was told that way back, thousands of years ago, there was a man that was sacrificed to a forked tree in order to live and in order to pray. When a man prays he should pray from the bottom of his heart, soul, body, and mind. You've got to sacrifice the water and the food. You might say you have to do penance; you suffer in there—you get dry and you get hungry, you get tired, you get sleepy. And sometimes a man has visions of the good things that are needed in life, or his people's needs. Now you take all these . . . the white people call them the medicine men—in former days they went out and they fasted. What visions they saw were brought home to help their people, not to ruin the people but to help the people to live, and support their people, and that still exists today—that's what the Sun Dance is for.

When I first went in, I had a son in the Marine corps, and I had about sixteen nephews in the armed forces. So I made up my mind I'd go in there and I'd pray for these—my son and my nephews—they can go through this war and come home to their homes. And it all come true. I didn't lose a nephew; I didn't lose a son.

Q   Does the cutting of the center pole and the cutting of the upright poles which go into the walls of the Sun Dance lodge go through a certain ritual or procedure?

A   The center pole, when a man goes out—a man that's putting on the Sun Dance—he goes out and looks for this tree, that's the center tree. When he finds one and says this is it, this is the one I'm going to use, then they go after that tree. Before they cut the tree they will pray with a pipe— pray to the Great Spirit that they want to use this tree to pray with, to fast with, and they want their prayers to come true—that's why they are using this tree. Wood was created for the betterment of a human being. Then they take this tree to where they are going to have the lodge. After digging the hollow, they pray again and they set up the center pole. The rest don't go through all that ceremony. That's just that one tree. Then they have one post right straight behind the center post and the forks are facing north and south. To the west of the center pole is a forked pole—a long pole with a fork at the end—that's the pole that the eagle sits on. That goes on first, doesn't take any ceremony or doings to put them up. After you get it all set up, you take the eagle and you pray to the Great Spirit. That represents the Great Spirit; you don't see the Great Spirit. That represents the Great Spirit, the eagle does.

Then the buffalo, you smoke on that, see, and you use cedar smudge. And they pray to that and tell the Great Spirit, well, the intention of this lodge being put up.

Q   And that's decided by the sponsor?

A   That's decided by the sponsor. He does the praying. Then he prays for all the people. I went to one last year, this summer, sponsored by Tom

Yellow Tail. There was a man who prayed for the Indians and prayed for the people of this nation. Now that's what a Sun Dance is for. And in order to have your prayers come true, you should sacrifice a little bit. That's the Indian religion where you sacrifice by fasting—you get tired, you don't eat, you don't drink water—and all you do is pray in there.

Q Do many people get visions of power during the Sun Dance any more?

A Well, they get visions; they still get visions. You might come in there, and I have seen white people in there, and they might pray for a certain thing, what their intention is, they might get a vision that that intention is accepted by the Great Spirit. You might have a vision of your family, how you are supposed to live. Some say it's a power given by the Great Spirit. There is one person, one creator; then there is the Great Spirit; then there is the son of the creator, as known by the American Indian from way back in time.

Q Does the coyote fit in the Sun Dance somehow?

A No, just the buffalo, the eagle, and the sun. The buffalo represents life—life of the American Indian.

In the early days the buffalo gave meat to the Indians to live physically, with the support of the Indian and his family, and the homes were made out of buffalo hides, the clothes were made out of buffalo hides, and the bedding was buffalo hides, everything that the Indian owned was from the buffalo. That was the life of the Indian, see. So that's what the buffalo represents in the Sun Dance.

Q Can you explain the difference between the creator and the Great Spirit and the son of the creator to me? Or do these all kind of flow together somehow?

A They are all in one. Now, you see, I'm a Catholic; in learning the teachings of the catechism they say Father, Son, and the Holy Spirit. That was known by the Indian before the white people came here. That is handed down mouth to mouth, that's the unwritten law of the American Indian. And the white people came along with their religion, and I notice that they don't live up to their religion.

Q When the people first go into the Sun Dance the first evening, could you explain how they actually go in?

A You see, the leader—you say the chief and the subchief—there are two leaders, but one is the main leader. The main leader goes around the hall once, he goes to the right. Then the other goes around the hall to the left. They make one round; when they come to the entrance to the hall— the entrance is wide—the main leader comes into the entrance on the right-hand post. Then he follows the room to this center pole as I was telling you about. The same way with the other leader, he comes to the left and he comes in and they meet at the center of the hall, straight west of the doorway. The door faces east. Then they all sit down and bring in what little bedding they have; they are barefooted. They are bare from the waist up and they sing four ceremony songs. After that, the man sponsoring the Sun Dance goes out and prays. He goes to the center pole and he prays, and after it gets real dark they build a fire in front of the center pole and there is a man that prays before he builds his fire.

Q   Does he have to have special qualifications to build a fire?

A   He's got to be a veteran of a war to build this fire and he tells a good deed—builds a fire and then calls on his clan uncles to pray for him. After that's done, the leader of the Sun Dance, this man sponsoring it, takes the cedar, puts it on the fire. After the cedar smokes, that's an offering to the Great Spirit, and he prays for the success of the Sun Dance; and he prays for the people that come in on the Sun Dance, prays for his singers and he prays for all the people. That's how it begins.

Q   When the two leaders come in, are they followed by the rest of their people?

A   Yes, they are followed by the rest of the participants.

Q   And then everybody stays in that same position in the lodge?

A   Same position for the whole three days. They go in—it's three nights—they go in in the evening, and they are in there the next day, the next night, and they are in there the next day and the next night, the third night. Then about noon some of them quit. Sometimes it goes to sundown, see, a full three days. But the Indian goes by the night, three nights.

Q   Does anything go on the first night after dark and after what you have already described?

A   After all these things are done, they start dancing. They sing four songs and the participants just stand there and whistle, blow their whistles made from the eagle's wing bone. The fourth song, the leaders start dancing and they dance up to the center pole, and they come back and then the rest begin to dance.

Q   Do they all do the same thing, or are they pretty much on their own?

A   They are pretty much on their own. You go in for certain reasons that are individual. They all face the center post, they all dance up to the center post and then back to where their bedding is or wherever they're standing, see.

Q   Do they ever turn their back on the center post?

A   Not while they are dancing. While you are dancing, you are facing the center pole, but if you are not singing, you can turn around; or if you are sitting down you can put your back to the center pole. They have singers all night and they dance all night, not all of them—some of them can rest if they want to, they can sleep.

Q   When people talk about singers in connection with a Sun Dance, do they mean singers who are not participants?

A   They are not—the other Crows that are on the outside are not participants with the dancers, and they come in and they sing for these people, and they are in groups, in teams. It's not one group that sings all the time. That's pretty hard to do. They might sing for two or three hours, and they get tired of singing and the other team comes in. And if that happens all night, why they dance all night. And if they're out of singers, why no more singers. You can go to bed, but you've got to get up before sunrise. And early in the morning they get up before sunrise, they are awakened by some of the older men that are in there.

There is one special song, the ceremony song that you dance facing the sun. You start dancing before the sun comes up, and then you dance until the sun comes up. While you are dancing, you are praying. And then after the sun comes up and the singers stop singing, then you sit around the fire and you sing four songs, ceremonial songs, and after each song you whistle four times. After that, the leader gets up and prays for the people; he puts on the cedar and he prays for the people, or he can call on some elderly person that's participating in the dance to do the praying. That's every morning, for the three mornings.

Generally, the second day is when the people come in to be prayed for. The sick people come in and want to be prayed for to get rid of their sickness. Maybe it takes all day, see people coming in. And there is one you might call the medicine man, you see the sponsoring person sometimes does not have the power to pray for the sick people, but he calls on somebody to do these things for him, see.

Q   And that takes someone who has the power to heal?

A   That's right.

Q   They don't do much dancing then?

A   Some of them, if they feel like dancing, they dance.

The second day is when they make the stalls. And the medicine men, they all come in with the feathers, you know, representing some power, but it's mostly the eagle feather.

Q   What is the significance of the stalls, if any?

A   You get weak, you've got to hang on to something to stand on your feet; you've got to brace yourself. They are upright—little trees like that. They are stuck in the ground. If I am sitting here, they have two for me. You might have to hold that to get up, and you will probably have to hold that to brace yourself.

Q   Is there any cover put over the top of the stalls?

A   No, just willows, tied with willows so you won't pull them over, see. The only cover you have is leaves; you got enough leaves you get in the shade; if you don't have enough leaves, why you just sit in the sun.

Q   Could you explain to me how they go about bringing out their medicine and doing that part of it?

Q   It all depends on the person, how he sees these things, or how it was told to him what to do. On mine, I doctor in there. There is an old man that prayed for me now, and told me that I wouldn't see any of these things until the next year, not to expect anything. That was the fifth time that I went in; towards spring I began to have visions on how to doctor people, what disease he has.

You go in the Sun Dance and maybe you will get a vision of somebody coming in, the power is going to tell you what the sickness of that person is, and it will probably tell you how to doctor him or how to pray for him or how to use the feather on him. That's the power that we were talking about. And not everybody has that power. I might hand it down to my son.

Q   You got your power through the visions?

A   That's right.

Q   Did you have to fast to get the visions?

A   That's right.

Q   Did you go out in the hills to do that?

A   No, I got in on the Sun Dance, fasted in the Sun Dance.

Q   Do the people paint themselves these days?

A   That's right. Our father is supposed to paint, see.

Q   And they get the instructions from visions?

A   That's right, from visions or from somebody that already has these powers. It might represent a bird, it might represent a buffalo—it all depends on the vision of this man that's painting. So each participant calls on their clan uncles to paint them if they want it, and if they don't want it, why they don't paint. All they do is just dance and pray. You're not supposed to wash your face but I see some here lately that do wash their faces with lotions, you know. I don't think it's right but they do it anyway. I don't do it.

Q   Do you know why they wash their faces?

A   I don't know. It's just something you learn from the white man, wash your face every morning. But during the fasting from times immemorial they don't touch water, even when they are fasting out in the hills. They come back, they go in the sweat tipi, go through the sweat tipi, and then they go into the water and they wash themselves off. But before they go out, they wash up, clean up, go into a sweat tipi, take a bath.

Q   In other words, you take a sweat bath before the Sun Dance and one afterwards.

A   Well, some of them do; I do that. I take sweat baths, wash up in the river—the best place is the running water. You might say you purify yourself before you go in.

Reservation life

Reservation Life

Reservation life means waiting. Here, the unemployed hope for jobs which are not readily available. There are few jobs at Rosebud aside from those provided by the Federal Government, or the tribe, in road construction or perhaps the Neighborhood Youth Corps and the like.

A major problem for Rosebud Tribal Chairman Webster Two Hawk and the councilmen (above) is the lack of adequate housing. Although the Federal Government has built some modern houses, some dwellings are still without running water.

The Rosebud Reservation.

The Rodeo.

The General Store.

Dance contests with cash prizes are the highlights of the powwows. In most of the Indian dances, women form a circle, moving in slow subtle steps; the men dance with more vibrant movements inside the circle, while drummers in the center sing in the Lakota language.

Felix White

Winnebago

Winnebago Reservation, Nebraska
Interviewed by Herbert T. Hoover
July 29, 1970

Mr. White is known among the people of his tribe for his
knowledge of Winnebago history. He was sixty-three years old
at the time of this interview.

FELIX WHITE   I was born in a wigwam down here about four miles on
the sixth day of July in 1907. And I lived in that area—sort of a Hiawatha
life, you might say, was enjoyed in my youthful days down there. I enjoyed
those days running through the woods, and was practically doing what
little boys used to do centuries ago. And if it wasn't for my mother I
would have completed my tests and so forth. She had been from the Iroquois
people and tribe—New York—educated at Carlisle, and she didn't believe
in her little boy going out and starving himself for four days and four
nights. She said, "He won't go without eating and will go upstairs and go
to bed, wash that face off." And so I didn't get to really complete the
ritualistic things the little boys go through to become a man . . . .

I went to school; I went to a grade school in Winnebago. Then I went
to the Genoa Indian School . . . . Then I went to Haskell to take electrical
engineering . . . . I went into stationary engineering. That's what training
the Government schools provided. I was student engineer at the school, and
by finishing the school I just went to the tenth grade. Well, then the superintendent there got me a position over in Toledo, Iowa, as assistant school
engineer. This was a sanitarium. I went there for a while, but then . . . this
power plant that I got in over here, there was this red button, and there
was a reset button on the circuit breaker, and I got curious. I always was a
curious one. So I said to myself, "Well, I'm here by myself; I'll push the
button." And something didn't work over there. I'm going to start finding

55

out about these things. The next thing, I was an electrical engineer. But I was denied that privilege at Haskell.

So I returned here to Winnebago and finished my high school work [in 1928] and wanted to go to Nebraska, but I didn't have any financial backing. I knew from the beginning I had to work my way, and so I got a scholarship at Junior College in Oklahoma, and I went down there. I graduated there in 1930. Then I went out East, and thought maybe I could get a scholarship. I made a chance at it anyway—football, lacrosse, and whatnot. And if I could just stretch the story just a little bit, I think I could have went maybe to Dartmouth. There was scholarships, I understood, for an outstanding young Indian that would qualify. I was a little late getting there. They already took the quotas for them. So that offered me an opportunity to go to Columbia University, which I went through in one day—in one side and out the back. Then I came back, thinking I would go to school some time and take some courses. Like I went to Omaha. I thought that between my jobs I might take a night course or something. You put it off, you never get it done.

I went back to school after that. I thought I might as well read. I was interested in medicine for a while there, until I was discouraged by some well-meaning doctors. And I thank them for it. They admired my grit and sand, to think I could work my way through medical school. But I am thankful for them setting me right, because if I finished medical school working my way, I wouldn't even be a good horse doctor. And what is the use of having a horse doctor when there ain't no horses? I would have missed the boat anyway, so I just went for the general art, the general course. I used to like to sing, and play football, and track, and dance, and so forth. So I'm not squawking. I had a nice time. We had hard times, at times. That's what we have to expect.

I was thinking of the 1832 treaty. The Winnebagos didn't want to give up any land, but they were somewhat forced. I used to wonder about it, so in searching the history books and laws and relations between the Government and the Indian tribes, and so forth, I came across a statement in one of the books that showed the 1832 treaty was negotiated by duress—the Battle of Bad Axe in 1832. Soon after, the treaty was made . . . . They were defeated a few days before that, see. Now in 1831, they [Government agents] were trying to negotiate a treaty with the Winnebagos for more territory and the Winnebagos didn't want to give it up. They said, "We don't want to give up our land." And while the negotiation was going on, why the settlers moved in. And the Indians happened to go on fall hunting trips up into northern Wisconsin. And the Sauk and Fox, along with the Winnebagos—which were friendly neighbors . . . they had quite a strong friendship—they went on their fall hunt. And in the spring of 1832, when they came back, this land or area someone was trying to make a treaty on was already surveyed and homes built and land being cleared and it was occupied—where before the treaty was made the non-Indians were supposed to stay out of it. I mean, they were encroached on all the time, and this started the Indians thinking that they had the right to drive them out. No treaty had been made. This was their property, and so in defense of their property they rose up, and the Sauk and Fox joined them, to drive out the intruders, not knowing there was an army post nearby. And so the battle didn't last too long. The most it was, was about three days or about four days. And so the treaty was made at Bad Axe.

HERBERT HOOVER Do you think Andrew Jackson was personally behind this policy?

A Well, as far as our history goes, in the history of the Five Civilized Tribes, and other tribes in the Southwest, his whole regime would bear out the fact that he was an Indian-hater. I mean, if they had civil-rights laws at that time they would have impeached him in a minute. I mean that maybe he meant well . . . but what he did was the thing we have to look at, to judge him on, or the pressures that made him do it . . . . There was a lot of pressure behind him, from people in the fashion of greed, and want, and so forth. And they put the excuse in there that progress must go on. I think progress cannot be stopped. But in order to proceed with progress, these people took in the way they did, which has a bad reflection on the country's history. And so they painfully neglected to put these facts in their history. If I was writing about this history, and my group had done something inhumane, without soul or some concern with the lives of people, I probably would try to camouflage this thing, too.

Q Was the 1837 treaty made under the same conditions?

A Yes. The President wanted to visit with and get acquainted with the Winnebagos, and the Winnebagos knew right off hand that this was another method of arriving at a treaty. So they questioned the Army representatives, who approached them about sending a delegation to Washington. And they said, "No." He [the President] just wants to give you gifts and get acquainted with you and so forth. And so the Winnebagos decided on who was to go. They did not send the required number of treaty-making personnel in this committee. They picked some people at random. Of course, they sent Chief Yellow Cloud, or Yellow Thunder, whatever his name was—he went along. And when they got down there, that was the first thing they started out with—to make this treaty in 1837. And this is the thing that bugs me. Now, in the 1832 treaty, they took the territory which they treatied for, and sort of in a way gave the Winnebagos more territory in the neutral grounds. That was in Iowa, Minnesota, plus four hundred thousand dollars, or thereabouts. They granted them 2,178,000 acres, in the neutral grounds. Then in a few years, I say five years later, they made the 1837 treaty, which took practically two-thirds of this newly established area back from occupation. You can hunt on it but you cannot occupy it. So what good is a deal if you cannot occupy it? Chief Justice Marshall said something about there shouldn't be any fraud or anything with the treating of Indians. I think there is a lot of laws and policies set up in the previous administrations, up to this treaty-making time, which would call upon the Government to deal fair . . . .

We got a big place to hunt, but we can't use it. Years ago Winnebagos of the way it used to be told to me that the guy that lived in the north, northeast corner, he wasn't even acquainted with anybody that was down in the southwest corner of the territory. They were somewhat strangers . . . . That was quite a territory at that time, and they sort of moved out. They wanted elbow room. They were not people for being squashed together in one place. That's why they had villages all over this area from Green Bay on down through Rock Island. They had little villages. Some made them by the name of the old man, the elder, who they just followed, and mainly set up a place—moved his family there to trap, or hunt, or something. Pretty soon other relatives came ,and they sort of had a village. They had a lot of room. They didn't believe in getting squashed into a small place.

Acting as a buffer between the Sioux and the Sauk and Fox people wasn't too healthy, either. See, you might be involved in something. So, they negotiated another treaty. And then, in fact, the land was too good for an Indian. One might put it that way. Some other guys come along there in covered wagons. "We could raise a lot of tall corn here," they say. So, strangers always pulled from some source to get what they wanted through legislation. So, prevailing upon them to make a treaty, the Government, they'll give you another place up in, oh, along Long Prairie, I guess it was— a little smaller. And from there, well, then it is too far north and the soil wasn't to the liking of the Winnebagos. It was too sandy, or something, to raise crops. They depended on the corn, and corn don't grow too good up there. So, then they decided to make another treaty and move down to the Blue Earth. That was nice. The Government decided that was too much land for the Winnebagos, however, so you better sell half of it. So, well, they made a treaty with the Indians and they said that this was good. So we would go along with it. So they sold part of it.

And pretty soon the [Santee] Sioux wanted to make war. And they come and asked the Winnebagos about joining them. They said, "No." They don't want no part of it. "We're at peace with the Great White Father, so we are not going to do it." But then the citizens of Minnesota didn't want any Indians in the state of Minnesota. "Get them out of here." The Winnebagos didn't have any part in the massacre, or in anything like that, in the war that went on. They had helped the Army apprehend the leaders of this thing here, and brought several of them to so-called justice, by dangling at the end of the rope. But even then they moved them out. So they put them through South Dakota and . . . they put them in the stockades . . . abuse and malnutrition and just plain unconcern about human life. And beatings took place there until they escaped. Many of them escaped, so they turned the rest of them loose. That's when they came to Nebraska. That was in 1863. And since then we've been here.

Jonas Keeble

Sisseton Sioux

Sisseton Reservation, South Dakota
Interviewed by Herbert T. Hoover
August 27, 1969

Jonas Keeble was educated at Genoa Indian School, worked as
a stone mason across South Dakota, and at retirement engaged
in "craft work to pass away time." Mr. Keeble was eighty-three
years old at the time of this interview.

JONAS KEEBLE   I was born at Pickerel Lake in an Indian tipi, and in
those days there was no hospital, but the mother was taken care of by her
own relatives . . . .

Now this is the Indian tipi. In my father's, mother's, and my grandfather's time the Indian tipi was sacred to them. They never played, or no
children would play in it. But to complete a tipi, they had to have twelve
poles for some reason, twelve of anything. [Four is a sacred number; this is
four three times.] They had pegs—to complete the tipi there had to be
forty. Well, everything is mentioned in forty in the Bible, too; everything
is forty. And then the canvas which held the tipi to complete it had to be
eight pins here, you see, and that means something. And then, one door,
and it always faced the east, and one rope holds the poles together and
comes down the center and nailed to the center to protect it from the storm,
to hold it tight to the ground. Now Grandfather said that the rope is from
above . . . .

I was baptized at St. James Church by Dr. Ashley, and Dr. Ashley is
the one that gave us the name "Keeble." In the beginning, Grandfather
was named Buffalo, but Father Ashley realized that it kind of sounded odd
to them, so Ashley gave us a name at baptism . . . .

When I was able to go to school, I went to Genoa, a big Indian school,
and that's where I got my trade. And in those days we had to sign up; our

parents had to sign up for three years. So I went to Genoa. It was a big Indian school, and was about four hundred boys there. So they had details and I would work as a carpenter one month and as a blacksmith for one month; and I would work at bricklaying for a month and work on a farm maybe a month. The detail they called it. So, after I got home, I was interested in bricklaying, so we done a lot of stone work all through the reservation. I worked everywhere, nearly, in South Dakota. Even that outfit that you passed by, that wall by the road, we built. And we built in Webster the Isaac Walton Club House with rocks. In those days there was my brothers, cousins, and my son; we stuck together, worked together, and we did some wonderful work—all over, even in North Dakota and around Aberdeen.

Besides the course in their way of doing business with a white man, it was taught to me in many ways in trading with the white man, see, like interpreter and prices of things, and we were also taught detective work.

I did a little detective work under a sheriff one time. Sam Bill. But those things seemed to be a secret way of teaching us, and by looking at a man, you could pretty near know what he is. By the fingerprints, finger-nails, and how he acts. Well, all that comes in that lesson . . . . So I went to the sheriff a lot of times and he used me as a detective lots of times, because I could understand young men, how they acted, and how they talked, and dispositions, and by looking at him in his face, if he was innocent.

I did quite a little hunting, quite a bit. There was more game at that time. And in those days our parents had no old-age pension, or any kind of help from the Government, except a payment in which they sell the land one time. And a man had to work and put up a cord of wood. There was plenty of wood at that time. So you could put up all the wood you could, and then the boss farmer comes and writes it down and takes it to the Indian office, you know, the first Indian office, the old agency. Well, they valued that cord, and then he gets rations for that. See, like blankets or sugar. In those days, there was no white sugar; there was brown sugar, and there was no decent flour, it was homemade grinding. And, of course, they got cloth. It wasn't up-to-date cloth, but it was cloth. And blankets, and so forth, Army blankets they called it. That's the way they made their living at one time.

What they had was just what they were hunting, like, you know, muskrats—and it was plentiful—and grouse. They were right in the trees. You could go right up and shoot all you wanted. Now, today there is nothing.

I trapped mink, muskrat, badger. In those days the fur was cheap, but it was a living. So I did lots of trapping, and a lot of hunting. I sold them at Waubay. It was a new town then. Muskrats were five to ten cents; now today you sell up to a dollar, and a dollar and a half. For mink you sometimes got two dollars; today, if there are any left, you get around thirty, forty dollars.

During 1908 I joined the state guard, the state militia they called it. I went to training. And there were a few boys, they are all passed away now. I think I'm the only one living today. Haydon died; and Charlie Bunker died; Alfred Barnes died. Four of us went to Fort Riley training, all the states sending their guards to Fort Riley at that time. There was no war; it was just a practice. I joined the state guard for three years, and at Fort Riley I was surprised at myself. There was a target, and you have to shoot against the other states; and I got second prize in marksmanship.

I remember when I was a boy, about five years old, I just remember a few settlers came along in Grenville, that's in Day County. And there was no railroad or store near enough to go to, so they had to journey clear to Watertown, to those stores at that time. And I remember Grandfather told me that he was out trapping muskrats, and he saw a dugout—smoke coming out—and he went up there to investigate and there was a settler moved in there. And they made a dugout, a few branches over the roof, you know, and a door. And he knocked at the door and a woman and a little boy came out. He got to meet my grandfather, and he made a statement so that he could understand this. Her husband went to Watertown for food, provisions, and he had been gone three days, and he went on foot. Grandfather asked them what he had to eat. He said, "We live on rutabagas until he comes back." So Grandfather went back and brought them—in those days the Government issued them food—brown sugar, grain, coffee, and so forth, dark flour. They hooked up the pony and took food up to the settlers. And this woman was so glad to get the food that she just cried, held him, and thanked him. Tears came out of his eyes because they were about starved. The husband hadn't come back yet.

I know the Indian way of life. We'll say when the Indians worked together they were always happy. They understood each other and they honored each other and whatever they had they earned by hunting. They had a chief and advisors with the chief for what is best for the tribe. And they had two. And one went out in the morning to announce to the people around the camp at daybreak. And this young man ordered the young men to do this and that. In order to gain a healthy way of life, you have to rise early and prepare your arrows and learn how to hunt, study the best and easiest ways to hunt. And one thing the young man is taught is that it is no way of old age to hunt, so when you get plenty, always remember the old age and throw the meat at the door and walk away. The old people come out and honor the young man who brought provisions for them.

The other one starts out later on, and advises the young ladies to honor their husbands, learn to make moccasins, learn to tan hides, and learn to prepare meat, because the food you get is given by the Great Spirit. He makes his rounds and goes into the center tipi and is given breakfast there. That's the way they lived at one time. So the Indian way of life at that time was different than it is today. Of course, it was a more civilized life. The Indian was already civilized; they knew what they were doing. They could take care of themselves their own way. They even had bodyguards. Nobody could do as they pleased—break the commandment. Why, you're forced out of camp and can never return. So they are prepared to stay with the tribe; why, they never want to do anything out of line. So that's the way they lived at one time.

Today, a girl or boy graduates, the Government never at one time gave them steady employment, and therefore they don't know what to do after they finish with high school. Now today they say we have a town, Sisseton. But I haven't seen any Indian or any young girl graduate clerk in a store yet that I know of. But you go off the reservation, like Eagle Butte. I went through there one time, and there was a couple of young men working at the garage. And I went to Jack & Jill store there, and there were a couple of girls working—clerks—working just the same as white girls. That's what I have seen on the other reservations.

I noticed that very few that went on relocation stayed and made good. Two that I know—Chris Gill, who went to California, I think it was. He owns a home and he's going to church down there and has a permanent job. He was a carpenter at the time he left. I had a daughter named Ada Howard that went to California during the Second World War and worked at welding, and she got married to a soldier boy and is still there yet. They got money in the bank, and they get along fine. That's two I know of, but most of them always come back—I don't know why—come back to the reservation. It's just a habit I guess or something; they come back and are unemployed.

I realize today, at my age now, that the Government never fulfilled its treaties. Now they have a payment pending since the last hundred years, and they talk about it every now and then. Even the CAP [Community Action Program] office questions, "What are you going to do with that money when you get it?" That the question. They asked an old lady what she was going to do with it. "Well, prepare my house or do something and I'd like to see that money while I'm living." Well, that's the way I feel. I'd like to use the money because it was given to us through our forefathers in a way, that we had coming, and the old age should get it without any consent; they should get it right away, and maybe the young people—it could be put away for them, for the future use . . . . I've heard that question for the last fifty years, but we never got it yet. And our attorney doesn't seem to do anything; he promised us and that's about as far as it goes. So what's holding the payment back, I don't know.

George Kills in Sight

Brule Sioux

Rosebud, South Dakota
Interviewed by Joseph H. Cash
Summer 1967

Mr. Kills in Sight is the chairman of the tribal land enterprise at
Rosebud. He was in his seventies at the time of this interview.

GEORGE KILLS IN SIGHT   Crazy Horse is sort of related to my grandmother on my father's side . . . a cousin. My grandfather, Big Crow, was
in the northern part of the state . . . what is now known as Cheyenne River
Reservation. He and the others were on a hunt. In the meantime members
of the Pine Ridge Indians went up there and told Crazy Horse that he's
wanted down to Fort Robinson. He kind of hesitates but finally they talk
him into it so they left. When that hunting party . . . come back they were
told, so right away . . . they followed them . . . almost a day behind. They
traveled at night too. Just about the time they came to Fort Robinson they
caught up with them. My grandfather had a six-shooter with a holster on.
"Brother-in-law," he said, "put this on. You may need it. Something is going
to happen." So he put it on his waist. They didn't go in with him. They
went so far and the guards stopped them.
     Those Pine Ridge members who went after him escorted him. Instead
of taking him to the army officer they take him right straight to the jail.
There are two guards on each side of him. The members of Pine Ridge
who escorted him told him that was the jail . . . in Indian. So he turned
around. His guard ran his bayonet through his guts. He didn't shoot him.
They just let him lay there . . . . The Pine Ridge claim he was their relation,
but if they had told him the truth he might not have gone there. They
must not have told him what they wanted. He took it for granted that they
just wanted to talk to him and this guard killed him.

My grandfather and his bunch claimed the body and they . . . made a travois and brought the body home to the camp where the northern Cheyenne were. His [Crazy Horse's] father and mother . . . bound him up in a buffalo robe tied with rawhide and wherever they go they take him along. They didn't bury him. The way they told it they had him almost a month. He was kept and he wasn't spoiled. The body was preserved.

They camped . . . on the Pine Ridge Reservation . . . now known as Manderson . . . right around the pines and breaks there . . . . They asked the father of Crazy Horse to bury his son. So he agreed to it. He was going to bury his son, but under one condition. He was to fill his pipe and those who would not ever tell where he was going to be buried will smoke the pipe with him . . . . They were pledged not to tell the place . . . . Those that were going to tell, they might as well leave because he is not going to bury him until they do. Just a few stayed and smoked the pipe. They dug a hole in a kind of washout . . . a ravine . . . close up to a ridge. They put the body in there and then put rocks just tight and put dirt on there and fix it so nobody ever think there is a grave. Those that were present at the time would never tell.

I had an uncle whose name was Coffee. Every spring or summer he went down there and visited the grave. He has . . . whetstones and knives that he [Crazy Horse] had. He had them but he didn't want to show them to anybody. He hid them in the badlands northeast of Parmalee. One day, I was working for the Government at the time, he sent word for me to take him over there, and he'll show me the place where he was buried. But he was too sick with pneumonia . . . he died soon after. Wherever he [Crazy Horse] is buried, a big cedar trees grows and it is right on the corner of a white man's land now. The southeast corner I believe he said. Nobody is alive that knows where he is buried and knows the whole story. My grandfather told me this story.

Crazy Horse was not a chief, but he was a medicine man. He was a real peace-loving man. The way my grandfather described him [he had] a kind of small build, real long coarse hair, and not a very attractive man. He was quite a medicine man. He could fix war bonnets where the man who wears the war bonnet gets into battle and never gets hit or wounded. [At the Battle of Little Big Horn] he sang his song and took sweet grass and tied it on his horse. He took the loose dirt from around a gopher hole and sprinkled it on the horse from his nose to his tail . . . . He went up right in front of Custer's dismounted cavalry and they started firing. He rode from one end to the other singing his medicine song. They think any minute his horse be shot down but he rode on through. He showed the black bullet marks on his skin . . . the bullets never went through.

Robert Morrison

Oglala Sioux

Rosebud Reservation, South Dakota
Interviewed by Joseph H. Cash
Summer 1967

Mr. Morrison, Holy Dance, was in his eighties at the time of this interview.

ROBERT MORRISON   Pine Ridge Boarding School—Red Cloud lives right across the creek from the school—and some of my folks are kind of kin to Red Cloud, so when I go someplace I go over there. His wife would make what the Indians call *wasna*. They dry beef jerky and they pound that, and they pound a lot of cherries with it, and they put a certain kind of grease with that and a little sugar, and they just mix that—the Indians call that *wasna*. I don't know what the whites call it. They've got a name for it, but I don't know. But she would do that and give us a little before we go back to school. Well, that's where I saw Red Cloud, and his wife, too.

JOSEPH H. CASH   What kind of fellow was he?

A   Well, he seems to be sort of a nice gentleman. He's partly blind, but he really talks nice to us kids, you know. He talked very nice. He was all right. Some of my folks were kin to him; some by the name of Steal Horse was kin to him. The Lamonts were kin to him. He had a lot of relatives there.

Q   You were in Pawnee Bill's show?

A   Yes, the Pawnee Bill Show. In the younger days, I was a young rider, you know. Wild West riding—wild horses and one thing and another. So I got in on that. I was with Texas Bill, too. And Buffalo Bill. I was about seven years old when I went to Philadelphia. I was there. I went with my grand-uncle. His name was Holy Dance. And I was just a little one, and he dressed me up in little Indian clothes and I went along.

Q   What did you get paid for it?

A I don't know. I was so small, I don't know how he paid. He paid my uncle there, my grand-uncle, he paid him. They didn't get very much then.

Q How much did you get when you were with Pawnee?

A Well, there I got a dollar a day and board. Sometimes I would ride the wild horses, and sometimes I would dress up in the old savage style, you know, and dance.

Paul Picotte

Yankton Sioux

Lake Andes, South Dakota
Interviewed by Joseph H. Cash
June 1968

Paul Picotte is regarded by Indians as the chief authority on tribal
history among the Yanktons. A graduate of Haskell Institute, he
is a descendant of the famed fur trader and Indian agent, Andrew
Drips. Mr. Picotte was eighty-eight years old at the time of this
interview.

JOSEPH H. CASH   What about Struck-by-the-Ree? What kind of man
was he? What can you remember about him?

PAUL PICOTTE   He was a wonderful man. He was born in 1804, right
down here west of Yankton, and Lewis and Clark were camped at Green
Island, that's six miles this side of Yankton over on the Nebraska side. They
were camped on this Green Island, and just as soon as they got set up with
their camp for the day, some of our Indian chiefs at that time went over
there and visited with them. And of course, Lewis and Clark gave them
medals and tobacco and one thing and another. The Yankton people were
very peaceable people. Anyway, they told Lewis that there was an Indian
baby born the day before. Well, he said, bring that baby over here. So
they took him over the next day, and Lewis wrapped him in an American
flag, and he never did raise a hand to revolt. And in the year of 1861 when
the Santee massacre—as they called it—between the Sisseton Indians and
the Santee tribe of the Sioux, they were having this uprising in 1861 in
Minnesota. They came down here and wanted old Struck to go up there
with him. He was chief of all the Indians. He wouldn't do it. He said, you
know, I never took the blood of a white man, and I never will. He had a
lot of influence, and I can remember the old man. I was only eight years
old. I went down to his little house. He used to sit outside there . . . . He

67

was a perfect gentleman. He was a model boy. He never drank any liquors of any kind, and he was always for something that was beneficial to the tribe. He always thought about somebody else. He's one of these fellows that if an Indian comes to his house, the first thing he does is give them something to eat, if it was nothing more than a little cup of coffee and a piece of crust. He was a wonderful man.

Henry Red Star

Sisseton Sioux

Sisseton Reservation, South Dakota
Interviewed by Herbert T. Hoover
August 27, 1969

Henry Red Star speaks little English, so the interview was conducted through interpreter Elijah Blackthunder. Mr. Red Star was
eighty-nine years old at the time of this interview.

ELIJAH BLACKTHUNDER When Mr. Red Star first remembers, what he
heard from his parents, they lived along the Minnesota River at St. Peter.
They came out here to hunt. Some came as far as Ortonville, some came
into this particular area, some came as far as Fort Sisseton, and some to
Brown's Valley. And that's where they got acquainted with this part of
the country.

There were seven bands; they all belonged to the same tribe. The
seven bands within the tribe had their own leaders; they called them
chiefs. And he said he remembers their names. At St. Peter, their chief
was Sleepy Eye; at Granite Falls, it was Running Water; at Montevideo,
the fellow that led the people was Red Iron; at Ortonville, their leader was
Red Feather Eagle; at Brown's Valley, Standing Buffalo; at Buffalo Lake, in
this area, Red Banner; and as Roslyn, Chase People was their leader. Mr.
Red Star was with the people who dwelled around Ortonville under the
leadership of Red Feather Eagle. As far as he remembers, he was born
right here at Buffalo Lake, August 15, 1880. He was with the Buffalo Lake
group.

When he was growing up, he remembers everybody grew corn and
potatoes. He says he didn't know who gave him the potatoes and corn to
plant, but they all had potatoes and corn . . . . When he was very young
. . . the Army gave them jobs to haul coal from Webster, which had the
main railroad at that time, . . . and they gave them as high as seven, eight

69

dollars a load for bringing the coal to Fort Sisseton. And they gave them groceries. And the Indians did the hauling—had to do it by oxen because there were no horses. They did it all by ox. [The oxen and wagons] belonged to the Indians . . . . He hunted quite a bit, shooting ducks and waterfowl and stuff like that, and he goes out and traps for furs—muskrats, skunks, and mink. In those years when he did his trapping, for muskrats he got seventy-five cents, and if it's an extra large one, he easily got about one dollar for it. And skunks in those days were worth three to four dollars. And a mink was worth fifteen dollars.

He said he wasn't the only one that did this thing here. There were quite a few people in his clan in those days that were doing the same thing. They went out and trapped and sold their pelts for whatever it was worth in those days. Usually they were sold for what the figures that he gave. The last time he hunted and trapped was back about twenty years ago. The people that had any furs or pelts to sell usually sold them in Sisseton, Lake City, Eden, or Waubay, as they were the neighboring towns of the Indian country.

The saddest thing that he can remember was the fact that a brother of his drowned on an island visible from here on a Sunday, April 15, 1886. They came to church in a boat from across the lake, and after church, going back again, they got within a short distance from the island there, and the boat capsized and his brother drowned.

Mr. Red Star went to school at Pierre Indian School, Goodwill Mission, and Santee Normal Training School. And he learned to be an organist, and can play both Indian music and English music. He can write the English language a little; not very much, but a little. Mr. Red Star also learned to figure a little arithmetic in the schools he went to. When he was going to school at these various places that he mentioned previously, the treatment was pretty rigid.

White people came into the Indian country in 1890, that is on this reservation, and were sold what he termed fraction acres of land. As far as he knows, the land deals were all straightforward, honest dealings. The white people bought these lands in good faith . . . . When the white people lived in Brown's Valley, they had coffee, flour, and other staples. And the white people wanted to trade this for buffalo hide and furs, pelts. The Indians needed groceries.

At the present time, he doesn't receive any help from any source. He only gets his rent payments . . . and he gets about twenty to twenty-five dollars a month. And then he goes out and works. He still works. He goes out and plasters the walls for people around here. That's his main job.

HERBERT HOOVER   Ask him how he was treated over the years by the Bureau of Indian Affairs.

A   The Bureau of Indian Affairs has been good to him personally, but some problems that come out of the Bureau are disheartening to a lot of people. And lots of Washington proposals to the tribe were very unfavorable for the people.

Q   What could the Government do that would help Indians today?

A   He thinks that if Washington would make it possible for more of the young people to get a better education—higher education—they could have good jobs and probably go into business for themselves. And by going into business for themselves, they would support themselves, as well as help the younger people to get more education, too.

They could, he thinks they should, have more business among the Indian people, to help one another go into businesses of their own. He understands that Washington will help other tribes with funds for young people to buy farm equipment to go farming. And if that could happen here, he thinks that more people would farm their own land, and help one another—provide jobs within the tribe.

Paul Picotte

Yankton Sioux

Lake Andes, South Dakota
Interviewed by Joseph H. Cash
June 1968

Paul Picotte is regarded by Indians as the chief authority on tribal
history among the Yanktons. A graduate of Haskell Institute, he
is a descendant of the famed fur trader and Indian agent, Andrew
Drips. Mr. Picotte was eighty-eight years old at the time of this
interview.

PAUL PICOTTE   Now in the early days of our Indian people here, as
well as Rosebud and Pine Ridge, under the treaty of 1858, the Government
was supposed to let our tribe select our own site for their administrative
purposes, which was down at Greenwood. Well, as time went on, the
lands on either side of Greenwood were flooded by the Missouri River in
the springtime, and that one spot never was flooded. They started a Government school down there at Greenwood, and there were two religious
organizations that were allocated by President Grant. There was a sort of a
fight between these various religious organizations to come in and try to
give the Indian people a little bit of religion. Well, Grant dedicated this
Yankton Reservation to the Episcopals and the Presbyterians; Holy Rosary,
Fort Yates, and Rosebud were allocated to the Catholics. As time went on,
of course, other religions came in there, but there was a time here when
our Catholic priest had to come through our reservation at night because
our administration down here had a mounted Indian police.

JOSEPH H. CASH   Did they ever catch him?

A   No—didn't catch him because they'd drive after night. Well, the
Picottes—mixed blood Indians—lived in a sort of a group, and he'd come
from Springfield with a horse and buggy, stop at our people, say his services there and stay that whole night. When the coast was clear, we'd let

him through, and he'd go on up here to Platte and a lot of those little inland towns up through there. He had a very big mission, which now doesn't seem very far, but at the same time, the population has increased so much that they have their own territories.

Up until 1899, I believe it was, all of our Government schools and the Episcopal parochial school were located at Greenwood. I went to school there in 1888 when I was only eight years old, and I knew old Struck-by-the Ree; I knew the gentleman, shook hands with him, and I have an enlarged picture of the old gentleman in the house. I've got his picture in there, from when he was the chief of our nation.

Well, anyway, on the other hand, with the Government schools, they didn't teach the children only up to the eighth grade. And along in the early nineties, some of us young fellows that had been to these schools and gotten up to the eighth grade, we had an opportunity to attend Haskell or Carlisle, and I for one in 1893 went down to Wabash, Indiana, and attended a Quaker school there. And the first year we were there, the Government got together with the Indian department, and they cut down the appropriations fifteen percent, so the board got together and decided to just close the school and make an old people's home out of it, which they did. So we fellows had a privilege then to be transferred to either one of these other schools that I mentioned.

Paul Robertson

Santee Sioux

Prairie Island Indian Community, Minnesota
Interviewed by Herbert T. Hoover
June 23, 1970

———————

Mr. Robertson was sixty-six years old at the time of this interview.

———————

PAUL ROBERTSON I was born in Cannonball, North Dakota. My parents were missionaries. My father was one of the first missionaries that was chosen to be sent out to speak the Good News among the western Dakotas—a Congregational missionary. And while they were there, I was born. There were about forty missionaries that were sent out from our church, and he was one of them . . . .

In 1833, as I was told, the Pawn brothers paddled up the Mississippi River to convert the Mississippi Sioux, and they successfully did their work. Later on, Dr. John P. Williamson came, and he was a missionary among the Sioux Indians. He was really a good missionary. He lived with the Sioux. He lived right with them, and ate together with them, and enjoyed pleasures with them. So at one time all the Mississippi Sioux were Presbyterian. But later a Congregational missionary came. His name was Thomas Long Lee Riggs. And there was Stephen Return Riggs. They came and organized the Congregational Church. So today there are many Congregational churches still going on.

I'm proud of the Sioux. First they lived in their own way. But when Christianity was presented to them, they accepted it, not only half-heartedly, but with honesty and in the truthful way that Christianity should be kept. They were all really dedicated Christians.

Soon after I was born, they [his parents] came back to the Santee Sioux Indian Reservation in Nebraska. I had five sisters and four brothers. And they were all sent to the Santee Normal Training School to receive their education. I was the only unfortunate one in the family. An ailment

74

which I had settled in my eyes. All my life, I had that eye ailment and I can't very well go out and earn myself a living. It's a good thing that my mother was a teacher. While I was unable to attend this school, she taught me at home. She taught me the alphabet and the numbers. And she taught me how to write my name and my address. Then, in the later years, when I was about fifteen or sixteen years old, I went to school—to a Government-supported school in Genoa, Nebraska. That was in the central part of Nebraska. I went at least five years. But most of the time I spent in the hospital trying to cure my eye ailment. It was unsuccessful. So the super-intendent had to call me into the main office one day, and he said that I should come home because of not being able to go to school anymore. So I came home, and since then I've never gone to school. I worked here and there as a harvest hand. And in later years I worked on the project called CCC, and WPA, and those Government programs. We planted trees, and maybe in wintertime we'd saw wood for old people—things like that. This was in the thirties when the Depression was in full-swing. Everybody had a hard time. I was lucky to get on that job.

When World War II came along, I worked out on the Union Pacific Railroad for a while, and also when I came back I went to work on the Norfolk, Nebraska Bridge Construction Company. Then, when I got done with that, there was an opening in the Union Pacific Railroad Company again, and I went back and worked for a while until I received a letter—my mother was sick in bed with a stroke. Then I had to come home and stay and help her out. So I didn't earn enough money for a social security retirement pension. I was unlucky all around. And yet, what little I learned I am making use of today. I am deacon of the Bazile Creek Congregational Church on the Santee Reservation.

My wife's folks here on the Prairie Island Indian Community have asked me to come and live with them. Of course, it's really hard to decide to say yes, because I love my church in Nebraska. But today, I've stayed here over one year now, I am beginning to get acquainted with all of the Indian folks here, the same as the white neighbors. And every chance I get I . . . speak here and there in the various clubs, like Kiwanis clubs, and Home Builders Association, and speak to elementary classes about Indian culture and traditions . . . .

I am working here with the Neighborhood Youth Corps. They work twenty-six hours a week. They get $1.45 an hour. They intend to clean up the powwow grounds for their upcoming powwow. I work with them—the headman for this Neighborhood Youth Corps . . . . Although I've never supervised any project like this, I'm doing the best I can, and we work together . . . . There are six workers right now, and one more wants to get in, but the requirements are that only six can work.

HERBERT HOOVER What do you remember from your childhood on the reservation?

A   In those days, the Government gave them—through treaties—they gave them horses, harness, and farming implements to farm with. And those early Indian farmers really did well, as I remember. I am very proud of the first Indian farmers. As I grew up, they had fairs—the Santee Indian Fair they called it. They had it at the end of August each year. It was no different from the county fair, because I have been to county fairs. They displayed all their exhibits—like raising potatoes, corn, beans, squash, and watermelon. All this they displayed. Even sewing—they made beautiful quilts. And these people were not educated. They didn't know a word of English, yet they did this. They also had on display poultry, swine, cattle, turkeys, ducks, all these things. They were really up there, the early Indian farmers.

Somehow the Government forgot about them, and that is the reason they seem to fall down in progress. Where they had made a good start, it faded away. So the Government, I guess, will have to start all over again, because there is a wide gap which will never be filled.

There was a school, too, supported by three churches—Episcopalian, Presbyterian, and Congregational. They supported Santee Normal Training School on the Santee Reservation. In the early 1930s a representative from the American Missionary Association came, though, and inspected it and decided that the buildings were all fire hazards. So the American Missionary Association board members decided to close it. And that's where the Christian ideals stopped also. Now, today, all the ordained ministers are dying off; just one or two or three Indian ministers are still living in that work.

If they had kept up that school, and if the Government kept up the teaching of Indians to be farmers, right where they had the good start— if they had continued, they would be better off today. The Government stopped its good work in 1922, I would imagine. They closed the Santee superintendent's office and discontinued the superintendent and all the other staff that the Government supported . . . .

I would like to say about the Government people, for instance, if any young white man is studying to be a doctor he is always being sent out to the Indian reservations. He would be stationed at an Indian reservation for maybe two years. Then, after that, he would be transferred to another reservation for two years, and another reservation . . . and so on. The experience is what this young doctor wants. And so I, myself, think that these reservations are the stepping stones for white men to become good doctors . . . . Then when he reaches the top, he is a professional doctor. Then he's sent out to where there are good businesses for him. And the experience that he received from these Indians reservations are really jewels to this young man. But the health conditions on the reservation are always the same—never been improved. In 1970, this is the way. Same way in the church work. Our Indian ministers have been retired, and some have passed away. And there are getting to be no more ministers. The high officials of the churches take young men from the eastern places, and place them in the Indian churches for experience, too. They would stay one place for a certain time, and transfer to another place for a certain time, and transfer to another. Then, when he reaches his required experience, he is ordained. Then he is sent off, too. And the Christian ideals on the reservation never improve; they're still the same way. Just like the Government did to the reservations when the physicians wanted to become professional doctors.

Neola Walker

Winnebago

Winnebago Reservation, Nebraska
Interviewed by Herbert T. Hoover
August 8, 1970

Mrs. Walker was forty years old at the time of this interview.

HERBERT HOOVER   How did Indian people, after they were placed on the reservation, make their livings?

NEOLA WALKER   Well, as far as the food goes, you know, Mother was a thrifty old girl. She did a lot of canning and preserving from the garden. And then when fruits were in season—blackberries, gooseberries, choke-cherries, plums, and strawberries—when they were in season, we went out. Mom was pretty crafty in the way that she would finangle to get us to do more work than we thought we should be doing. We had candy and things like that, you know, like my kids now. But out home, we seldom had candy, and the little extras. And she would stash them someplace, and then when it came berrypicking time, whoever picked the most would get an extra piece of candy. We all got a piece, but the one that picked the most would get the extra. And then after we got home, you had to stem the gooseberries, you know, so she would put a bowl full in front of us. And we had a big old blanket on the ground like that. Then she put a bowl in front of each of us, and we'd have to sit there and stem them. Whoever got done first got the extra piece of candy. Yeah, she was pretty sly the way she used to work. She made things fun for us, you know, so we were working but we didn't really realize it.

Q   You said your father cut wood?

A   Yes, they use to cut posts—he and Mom both—and sell them. At the time, they hardly got anything for them. Locally, they were getting less than ten cents, but at Emerson and Homer and the surrounding towns, they got fifteen cents, and like that. I think the most anybody ever got was about a quarter a post. And that was later—in the forties, when the prices went up.

They had the horse and wagon to haul all of these. They would go clear down to timbers there. We lived about eight miles west of town, so they would start off early in the morning, about four o'clock, and they would go down about fifteen miles in the wagon. They'd get down the timbers and cut all day and load up about dark, and then start home. They had a friend who lived in town; they'd park the posts there, and sell it from there. But my dad used to sell quite a bit of his out toward Emerson, further west. That was the only industry really around here, where they got any money. And that was good money for the times, I guess.

They'd do a little hunting. When I was younger, there was no deer around. There was mostly just rabbits, small game, and pheasants, and ducks. Some of the families did quite a bit of fishing, and they would take them down and sell them to the other families who didn't fish. But it has just been recently that the deer came down here. They haven't always been here.

Q   What about your early education?

A   While I was quite small, I stayed at the Reform Mission. My mother and father moved back, back out on the farm during the school year, in the spring of the year, so they put us up at the Reform Mission. We had to talk Indian at home, and then, when you saw an Indian kid, you just naturally talked Indian. But there they whipped you if you didn't speak English. And some of the children who went to school up there couldn't speak a word of English. Say they were ten years old and they still were just starting school; they would get whippings for talking Indian. And for anything Indian, you were beaten; they used big long rubber hoses, about two or three feet long. They would take heavy boards and crack them across the knuckles.

The Dutch people around the mission said that it was a sin to dance, and so if they caught you even going through the motion, like making off you were going to dance, you'd get a whipping. I always thought to myself, "My folks danced . . . . And so I could dance." It wasn't wrong to dance. And it wasn't wrong to talk Indian. That's the only way I could talk to my grandma and them. So I just made up my mind I was going to talk Indian.

Paul Picotte

Yankton Sioux

Lake Andes, South Dakota
Interviewed by Joseph H. Cash
June 1968

Paul Picotte is regarded by Indians as the chief authority on tribal
history among the Yanktons. A graduate of Haskell Institute, he
is a descendant of the famed fur trader and Indian agent, Andrew
Drips. Mr. Picotte was eighty-eight years old at the time of this
interview.

PAUL PICOTTE   We lived right down there north of Marty, and he [my
father] farmed about a forty-acre tract, and he dug his own well there;
and we raised chickens, and Mother had a good garden. Of course, my
mother was only a quarter Indian. And we had fruit trees and a couple
of cows to milk, raised hogs and stuff like that. But the fullblood Indians
that belonged to those dance outfits, they would maneuver around some
way, and get hold of a hog or calf or something and give a feast, and all
come to their place and have a plowing bee. And they'd plow up that
fellow's land, and the women would go along and plant it by hand. They'd
fix up their dress some way, and put the corn in there and a sharp stick
down that way, and they'd stick that in there and would go right down
the field. They'd plow that field and plant it, all at one time. And the next
guy, he'd get ahold of something to eat, and they'd go over there and camp
and do the plowing there. Well, that's the way they did it there. But my
dad never did do that. He farmed for himself.

We were set here in 1859, and prior to that time our Indian people
depended altogether on the buffalo hunt. The last buffalo that was killed—
there were seven of them located over here about twenty miles west of
here—they got six of them, and the last one they got in about 1869. That's
the last buffalo killed on this reservation—just out of town here a little

ways, about a mile and a half. In the earlier days, two hundred years ago, this valley going down here between here and Pickstown was known as the Gate of the Buffalo. In the late fall, November and December, all these potholes out across here were just full of buffalo. When those things would freeze up and there wasn't any water, they'd get together by the thousands and come down in through here because right down in there were springs in the Missouri River. They'd stampede down in there, and many of them drowned.

Those Indian people had a regular program. No one private Indian could go out and kill a buffalo unless they went together. This old chief had his various lieutenants, and he would send them out to locate these buffalo from these various lookout points, and wherever they located those buffalo, then they'd have a meeting there. He'd come back and make his report, they'd have a meeting there, and then they'd go out as a unit, try to surround those buffalo and get all of them. And then they would camp. They'd move their camp up there on the grounds, and then they would set up some forked poles about like that, you know, and then put some across that way. They'd cut up all this meat in pieces about that thick, probably eight, ten feet long, and hang them over these poles and let them dry, let that meat dry. There were no flies, there were no potato bugs—even during my time in the early days. We didn't have flies until these white fellows came here. Anyway, those Indian people would take this meat after it was cured, and they'd go down to the river, pretty close there, and they'd cut this hay there. I saw some of that bottom grass just this morning. It grows about so high.

JOSEPH H. CASH   About three or four feet high?

A   Yes, all of that. There's some of that along the road going down to Greenwood. They'd cut that with their knives, they didn't have anything else. They'd cut that with their knives and lay it to one side, and then they'd cut the ground out in sections and lay that over to one side. Then they'd dig up this earth and the Indian women would put it in their dresses and haul it over to the river and empty it in the river. They'd dig a pit there three, four feet across and maybe five or six feet deep. Then they'd put a layer of this straw down there, and a layer of this dry meat, so it wasn't touching one another; then they'd put another layer of grass, and so on, until they filled it all up, and then they'd kind of tamp that down a little bit and put some more hay on the top. Then they'd go get the tops of the grass there, blocks of dirt, and they'd place that just the way they took it out. Then they'd go over there so far away and they'd blaze a tree, and the camp would move on to the next buffalo hunting stop. In the meantime, these lookout fellows would be on duty, going out there trying to locate more buffalo. When fall came, they'd move down to their first cache. They were right close to the river where they could get water and wood and set their camp up. They slept right on the ground; they were healthy . . . .

She's [my grandmother] the one that gave me all of this history, because she was a pretty progressive old Indian lady, and she knew the Indian ways and all that stuff, and she gave me that history . . . .

Whenever that cache run out, why they'd move down to the next one, and so on down the line. And then spring would come, and the buffalo would go back out on the green grass, why, they'd go out on their buffalo hunts and do the same thing again. Some of the older people would station themselves along the Missouri River where they had access to the river water and the wood and plenty of stuff to eat, and they would spade up a little piece of ground there and plant maize, this Indian corn.

Q   The Yankton Indians apparently never gave up farming, at least growing corn, completely like the ones that went out West?

A   No, no. And not only that, they took advantage of all the wild fruit that grew on our river bottom here, you know. There were wild plums and wild cherries, and wild buffalo berries and other plants that they could use. Wild onions, and they'd take those and dry them. Then they'd go out on the prairies and dig up these wild Indian turnips, and they would peel those things and make a braid out of them. They'd braid maybe forty or fifty of them and hang them over a pole and they'd dry. In the winter months, they'd take that corn, they'd pound that all up; they'd take the cherries and they'd pound them up in patties about like that, and dry them. And they would mix that together, and mix a buffalo tallow with that, and they had something that was just out of this world. Healthy . . . .

No salt, no sugar, no flour. And in 1859 when they were first moved here at Greenwood under Major Redfield—or Redpath—they issued the Indians some commodities, and among other things in those commodities was flour, and they taught the Indians how to use that, and they'd just cook their bread right on top of the stove, you know.

And then they issued them some salt pork. And you know what the Indians done with that? They threw it in the river.

Titus Goodbird

Sisseton Sioux

Sisseton, South Dakota
Interviewed by Herbert T. Hoover
August 28, 1969

Titus Goodbird spoke English with difficulty, so the interview was
conducted through interpreter Elijah Blackthunder. Mr. Goodbird
was seventy-nine years old at the time of this interview.

ELIJAH BLACKTHUNDER   Mr. Goodbird was born in Marshall County in
1890. He went to school at Goodwill. He said he didn't go to school very
long—he only went about three years. For the fact he was only there a short
time, he didn't learn very much. He says that at that school, Goodwill out
here, there are quite a few missionaries, priests, and quite a few people
that learned to play the organ. They turned out to be good musicians.

During the uprising [of 1862] lots of people fled from the riot area.
Lots of people went . . . . His family—his grandfather, father and himself,
and his relatives—they're the ones that didn't go along. They stayed seven
miles northeast of Redfield, South Dakota. They never went along. His
father and family lived at what is called Big Lake, west of here. And his
father planted quite a lot of things—such as wheat, potatoes, corn, beans,
and everything. He said they always lived real good. They done a lot of
hunting and everything, such as ducks and so forth. And they also trapped.
They trapped mink, muskrats, badger, weasel, anything that had fur, that
they could sell. The mink at that time was worth about ten dollars or less,
and the muskrats were sold for ten cents each, or somewhere in that neighborhood. And the badgers sold for five dollars. The weasel brought about
seventy-five cents.

Most of the time they cut and sold wood . . . and this wood that they
sold, a cord was four dollars, and an oak cord sold for about six or eight

dollars, or somewhere around in there. And then the fence posts, they sold for ten cents or somewhere around in that neighborhood.

The corn that they raised was mostly what they call Indian corn, and that's for their own use. The ate that whenever they felt like eating corn. When they hunted for meat to eat, usually they ate the muskrat meat and rabbit. At that time they didn't think there was any deer around here. They also hunted prairie chicken. And then, of course, the ducks were plentiful . . . . They always fished and ate the fish, too. There was no such thing as help from the Government, as far as food was concerned, in those days.

Most of the white people were living in the Brown's Valley area, and they just came in and claimed certain tracts here and there. That's why they got in. He never heard of any payments for the land that they took when they came in from Brown's Valley area and settled in here. He said he never heard of any settlement of any kind.

His grandfather . . . Mitchell Paul, he's the person that mapped out this reservation. Not particularly mapped out, but he made the lines when the reservation was made. For this great deed of making reservation boundary lines, the Government has put up a metal grave marker for his grave at Long Hollow, a church up here west of Sisseton.

HERBERT HOOVER   Does he remember anything about Chief Renville?

A   Chief Renville's English name was Victor Renville. And his Indian name was Ohiye. He was particularly helpful in keeping the Indians from getting rid of their land. Maybe some tried to sell their land, but he always advised against it, and he said his help in that particular way was real good because today there is some Indian land left for the people now, and for the younger people coming up.

Q   Is the Government helpful to Indians on this reservation?

A   He thinks that if the Government would provide assistance in maintaining individual families outside of town, in their various localities—original localities, from which they came—and if they provided such things as horses, and things to work with, the Indians would live better than they do here in town.

For the younger men who are able to work, it would be better for them to relocate somewhere else, where there are more job opportunities and work, and make their own living and provide for themselves. But for the ones that can't leave here at all, it's not good as far as work is concerned, because there are no jobs whatever here around this territory.

The personal thing that bothers most of them is the fact that Indians today are somewhat like the former slaves of the South. They're somewhat like being in jail. They can't do nothing for themselves. They have superiors over them, and the authority from the superintendent. Everything is pretty well controlled by local authorities so that individuals can't do as they would like to do. They have to get consent from the superiors for everything they want to do. They have to ask, and they say "No." Well, that's it. Most of the time whatever we ask, it's "No."

Q   What kind of income does Mr. Goodbird have?

A   The only help he gets now is his old-age pension. It's thirty-two dollars. His wife gets thirty dollars. All together, for rent money and so on, they get about eighty dollars a month.

Henrietta Chief

Winnebago

Winnebago Reservation, Nebraska
Interviewed by Herbert T. Hoover
August 7, 1970

Mrs. Chief was seventy-six years old at the time of this interview.

HENRIETTA CHIEF I must have been about eight years old when they took us. My father and mother had parted, and I guess my mom couldn't take care of us all. And there were three of us, and the Government, you know, they come and they took us to the Tomah Indian School. And that's where we were raised. I was there for about nine years. And about thirteen, fourteen, right in there, fifteen—I don't know which it was, how old I was then—and that's when I was first converted. The superintendent showed slides—that was before moving pictures—he showed slides, and he showed Jesus on the cross with His arms outstretched, you know, like that. Right then and there I accepted Jesus as my Lord and Saviour. That's been over sixty years. And I'm happy, just as I was when I was converted . . . .

I just went as far as eighth grade. Just studied arithmetic and English, and read, you know, and we used to write home letters. My mother and my father used to write us . . . . Oh, I just loved that school, because that's where I was converted. And he was just like a minister, our superintendent. I heard he passed away, Mr. Compton; Allen Compton his name was. And I have no regrets. I had three square meals a day. The Government helped me there again. They helped all the time, and they had cattle there . , . they had a herd of cattle there and they had all the milk we wanted and chickens—they raised chickens. And I just went as far as the eighth grade and we came down here . . . .

My mother—my father had passed away—remarried and started raising a family by my stepfather and sent for us from there. And then we were all again in a surrey or something and . . . [they] put us on a train there and we rode all night and got to Sioux City early in the morning . . . . It was raining when we got here—1908 that was. And my dad [said] . . . the first thing, "Oh, my little girls came back," he said, and shook hands with us. That was my stepfather. He is just like a father to me . . . if I did anything wrong he would talk real good to me and tell me that is wrong, but he never did come out and never said a cross word to me . . . .

Then in 1911 my husband and I were married . . . . And I got married the old Bible way. And you know, I read in some part where the father and the mother, they picked their daughter or son's mates for life. Well, I listened to my father and mother. They picked my partner for life and we celebrated our fiftieth wedding anniversary, John and I. He passed away in 1962 . . . .

HERBERT HOOVER   Do you remember much about the 1930s, the Depression years?

A   Oh, yes I do. I know we had a hard time there, real hard time, my husband and I, in the Depression years. I remember one time, I don't know how come little George woke, I remember our little ones didn't have hardly anything to eat. And I remember my husband, he just had a dollar or twenty-five cents or something, at the store. There used to be a little store at the agency . . . . We couldn't sell him anything and here my cousin George Wolf, he had just come back from Wisconsin and he was at the store, and he asked him [my husband] what he was in the store for, and he said, "I just came to get a little something." And he said, "You go on back," he said, "I'll get you something to eat." He had someone's buggy there at the agency. He came in and my husband said, "I saw George, he just came back from Wisconsin, and he said he will get something to eat." Oh, I was just so happy . . . .

I was baptized in the Episcopal Church in 1907 in Wisconsin, Tomah. When I came down here, or when we came down here, the church had just become the Reformed Church, and Reverend Wadenaldo was here. He just came, too, that year, 1908, and he asked me. Well, I couldn't come to church here in town, the Episcopal, because sometimes it would rain and we didn't have cars them days, and we couldn't come with horses . . . . We went to church right at the agency. The Reformed Church was there then at the agency so I just went there . . . . I told him I was baptized in the Episcopal Church and he said . . . "I don't want to ask you to join us, but if you want to we'd like to have you join us. And if you don't," he says, "I'm going to ask you to help me with my church work." So ever since 1908 I have been helping in the Reformed Church here . . . .

Q   When you were small, you said you went to see Ringling Brothers.

A   My uncle took us to a Ringling Brothers show. We started out early in the morning, way down from these timbers here, and we started before sunrise, way before sunrise with a team and a little wagon. And we got to South Sioux in the evening just to get there. When we got there, and we was going to go to the show the next day, they pitched the tent up there by the river, by the river by Sioux City, and my aunt cooked and we had supper and there was not one building there . . . . They used to take us to shows like that, and a woman told my fortune one time.

Q   Did the circus ever come out to the reservation?

A   No, I don't remember.

Q   Did you have other types of entertainment when you were young?

A   Oh, I know I used to crawl over the snow. Yeah, and I never noticed the cold at all . . . . But in those days, I must have been raised real good, because I remember we ate oatmeal—oatmeal every morning—and eggs, we had eggs . . . . We played games, and I remember one time, the Fourth of July, they used to have fireworks there.

Q   Did you have a doctor then?

A   Yes, we used to have the Government doctors. We used to have, at the agency you know, and the hospital used to be out there—the Government hospital. Had the Government hospital, and yeah, ol' Uncle Sam, he was pretty good to us. Some kicked, but I don't.

Sam Robertson

Sisseton Sioux

Sisseton Reservation, South Dakota
Interviewed by Herbert T. Hoover
August 26, 1969

———

Mr. Robertson was ninety-three years old at the time of this interview.

———

SAM ROBERTSON   Well, the first I remember, when I was three years old, I saw a train. That was down at Breckenridge, Minnesota. And lots of Indians went down there with us. Nobody talked English in this territory, on this reservation. Just a few of them talked English, and my dad talked both English and Indian. My dad is only one-eighth Indian, and the rest is Scotch, but he talked just as good as we can, the Sioux language. And when he went to town, about twelve or fifteen wagons followed him. On this reservation, all the Indians were farmers, using a walking plow, sowing by hand. Some of them harvested, cut wheat by hand. And they had only one threshing machine. It was my grandpa's, my mother's father. He was a full-blood Indian. I don't know why he worked like that. He bought this threshing machine, and he had a fifty—farmed fifty acres. That's the biggest farm on this reservation. The rest of them are only fifteen, twenty, twenty-five, thirty, thirty-five, some of them forty. But fifty acres is the biggest farm on this reservation at that time.

And when my dad went, they'd all go with him. They had to stay there one day at Breckenridge; that's the closest railroad that we had, and that's the only place they can sell their wheat. So, they all had to take a load of wheat in the fall when they went. They followed him that far, and then of course we got home. There wasn't much money, but they all had something to eat. They all had a garden, milk, one or two cows in each family; the Government issued cows, you know. So they milked cows and

89

raised chickens. A few of them had pigs. Of course, my dad, he's just like a white man. He had everything—pigs, cattle, horses, everything he could have. That's the way they got along at that time. Some of them got along pretty good, farmed pretty good, took care of this stuff pretty good. Nobody drank at that time. And they couldn't bring any whiskey inside the reservation, not a drop. That's a rule they had. They made that themselves with the Government in the 1867 treaty.

In 1873, before I was born, they put up this old agency. The Government built an agency here, and we were supposed to have an agent. And they sent a man from Washington for our agent; now they call it superintendent. Our agent came, and he had to get all the Indians together at the office, and he told them what he was going to do. He told them they sent him from Washington to the agency to take care of the people here. But they didn't give him any rules, law or anything. "We have a law," he said, "I'm going to use that and we're all going to use it." "That's the Ten Commandments. If you break one of these, you'll be in a jail here—that stone house. You stayed there about ten days, maybe fifteen days." Now that's the way he started the people.

First thing you know, he said, "You chop all the wood for Sunday, pile it up in front of the door for Sunday; bring the axe inside the house and just lay it there and don't touch it until Monday." And the people did. And on Sunday, everybody would go to church; whoever had a church would go to it. And then we'd do nothing, just go to church and come back. If some families didn't want to get into company and visiting, they might have a deck of cards at home, and play cards on Sunday. And sit down here in the jail ten days. So they used that Sunday the way they ought to use it at that time. This is from 1873 until I was born, and maybe even until I was three years old. I remember we all went to church every Sunday. My father was the lay-reader. They made him read at the Episcopal Church. He had a service about half a mile from our place. We had to walk over there—we used to walk with my father when I was four years old. That's the way the people got along. Everybody would help each other; and the men were just like brothers and the ladies all like sisters. Everybody helped each other. If somebody wanted to do something he couldn't handle, they would all go over and finish that for him. They didn't charge him a dollar an hour either. It was free. Well, that's the way we got along until we got mixed up with the white folks; then Sundays went away. The white men went to work on Sundays. And they would bring this whiskey, and whiskey put us where we are now.

Every family on this reservation farmed. Some of them got along pretty good. They put up all the hay they could, that they were going to use, and they raised feed. My dad, he farmed fifty acres, and he would get a good crop, all the time until 1887. Then no rain came for seven years, up to 1894. Wheat would grow only five to six bushels to the acre. And the price was only forty cents a bushel at that time. The white man can always remember that, you know, Cleveland times they say, Democrats.

Still the Indians got along pretty good. Some of them had a farm they didn't farm much, you know. They had about a hundred bushels of wheat, some of them one hundred and fifty, some of them two hundred bushels. But they had a flour mill down at Lidgerwood, North Dakota. They'd take the wheat over there and bring home whatever they could use. My daddy always brought home sixteen hundred pounds of flour once a year, in the fall. He'd take it over there and exchange his wheat, you see. Every bushel, he'd take thirty-three pounds of flour. But he just got the flour once a year. Mother had a big frame house. He didn't get the lumber from outside either; he cut these big trees, you know, big oak trees. Bring them down to the agency. The Government had a saw mill at that time. He kept on hauling that lumber, those logs, down here until he had enough lumber to build a house. The house is still standing there yet—all oak two-by-fours and sixes. Even the rough boards are oak. But he had to buy the shingles for the roof, and the siding.

You see, we never had a white man in this area, for a long time. They lived outside the reservation, the white men all around here. They're the ones that got a hard time. They all had all kinds to eat—big garden, lots of pigs, sheep, chickens, turkeys, and geese, milked lots of cows. They didn't have to buy any milk or any butter; they all had plenty of butter. That's the way they got along outside this reservation. But they had nothing to burn. Some of them burned manure. But then the white man would come in, you know, and the Indians had all this wood clear up into North Dakota. Both Indians and white men would butcher pigs or cows or whatever they wanted to butcher. And they would bring it up and trade it off for wood. You could load all you wanted on your wagon for $2.50. We traded and figured out how much the meat was worth, and the wood and everything. The white man and Indian got along just like they were brothers. They got along good. The white men got the wood. The Indian helped the white man, and they got help from the white man—meat, pork, anything you wanted. Turkey, how many turkeys you wanted. That's the way they got along. Now they don't get along very well, I don't think.

Back in 1851 they marked this reservation, and outside clear up to the Missouri River, clear up to the Canadian line, clear up the Minnesota line. Outside this reservation, they sold that land for ten cents an acre. But it wasn't surveyed, you know. The Government thought there was about eight million acres, and he paid for eight million acres at ten cents an acre for the land. After they measured it up, it was eleven million acres, so the Government made big money on us—they got all that land for nothing, never paid for it. I guess they have to pay it now, but I don't know when they're going to pay.

The Government and these smart white fellows, you know, white men wanted to get some of this land inside this reservation, too. So they went to work and gave us a chance to sell our land. I didn't want any deed to my land, but they gave me my deed to the land anyway. That's when it started, in 1911, I think. And that's the way they got all our land. Some of them (before they got deeds for the land, the white man knew that's how he's going to get the deed) let them have $1,000, you know, make a loan, $1,000 on the land. The Indian didn't have any way to pay that $1,000, so they took 160 acres for $1,000, and it's good land, too.

My uncle, he trusted this fellow, you know. He's a banker, this fellow that's going to buy land. He says, "Angus, I ain't got enough money," and he's working in the bank. "But I'll give you $80 an acre for that 80 acres. And I'm going to pay you $2,000 down, and then I'll give you so much every year, maybe $2,000 a year or something like that." So my uncle, he says, "You have to put your mortgage on that, you know, security on that." That was all right. So they made it out that way. It went along there, and he never paid anything. So one day my uncle went up there into the bank and (he lived only about a mile and a half from town) he says, "Ed, you got to pay now. I want the money." Well, he didn't answer him just exactly right, and my uncle said, "If you don't pay anything I'm going to foreclose on you; I'm going to take my land back." Well, that fellow he didn't say much. So my uncle went to the law, and he was going to foreclose on him. Here he had $3,000 against him. This fellow went down to Sisseton and made a loan on $3,000, so my dad and my uncle had only second mortgages. See, the other fellow got four sections. So my uncle lost that land. That's the way they use us. So my uncle got his first payment; that's all he got for his 80 acres. He didn't get $80 an acre.

Some superintendents, they stick up for the Indians. But not all of them; just a few of them. Of course, they are all white men, and they all stick together. They don't stick up for the Indian, but they stick up for the white, you see. They're the ones that make lots of crooked deals. Some of the superintendents didn't know it. Some knew it, but they don't like to do anything. Like in Sisseton, all those big shots in Sisseton, they got lots of land from the Indians for just about nothing. And the superintendent knew it but he let them go. That's the way they use us.

HERBERT HOOVER   What did you do during the Depression?

A   I walked 1280 miles the summer of 1934, from the first of June to November fourth. I was on a gopher project, $2.10 a day. That's the money I got, that's what I walked for. From the first of June up to November fourth, I walked 1280 miles. We poisoned flickertails, and then after the first of September we poisoned pocket gophers. And we kept that going until the ground froze up, and we had to quit because we couldn't make a hole in the dirt then.

Q   Where were you educated?

A   I got no education. I went to school when I was twelve years old, down here at the Government school. When we eat at home, we eat good all the time. But at the school we had oatmeal and molasses for breakfast, and sour bread. They baked the bread right there, and we got sour. We all have a stomach-ache every day. Then we had meat once a day at dinner time. In the evening, they cut the meat all up in two boilers with the cover on, and they had that on a big stove. The fireman, you know, he kept that fire going all night, boiling all night until morning. That meat is all boiled to pieces. And they lay it on the one side there and it stands there until dinner time when they're ready to eat it; it would be sour. They gave it to us. She—the cook—didn't care. So we all had stomach-aches.

Many of us came that couldn't talk English. That's for sure. That fellow would come in, and he'd call us by our names and say, "Come in here." We got in the teacher's room. I remember that fellow's name, too—John McClennan. He sat in a chair, and the book. Well, he would come around, and open up our books. And he would say, "All right, we start." We stated just what he said; we never looked at the book, just watched him. When he got through with the book, "All right, go back and take your seat." He didn't make us spell, or anything. We went on like that for two years. I went to school only eighteen months. That's all I went to school. I never could figure anything; he never made us figure. The last year I was there, two girls from McCullough, teachers, they're the ones that made us spell, made us talk and write, and made us figure stuff—the last year I was there. And then my dad took me off, and I never went back to school. I went home. I was eleven, twelve years old, and I helped my dad with the farming. When I was thirteen years old, I would use a plow, a walking plow. I would do all the dragging. And my dad would do all the sowing by hand. I worked at home.

Mildred Stinson

Oglala Sioux

Rapid City, South Dakota
Interviewed by M. Edward McGaa
Summer 1968

Mrs. Stinson was fifty-five years old at the time of this interview.

MILDRED STINSON My name is Mildred McGaa Stinson. I was born at a place called Godfrey Springs on the Pine Ridge Reservation. I'm an Oglala Sioux. I'm fifty-five years old now.

My grandparents—we only lived a fourth of a mile from my grandparents; and it was nothing, every day, sometimes two and three times a day, we would go down, back and forth. It was just like our own home; we had love. All my uncles would pick us up and hug us and love us, and aunts; and then we would go over to my mother's side who were more the fullblood Indian type. We would go up there, maybe a week at a time to visit all around. And I remember my old grand-aunts would love us; I mean there was kindness and love—and they would pat us, maybe give us an extra piece of bread or something you wanted, asked you if you wanted this or you wanted that. And sitting, all the uncles would cross their legs and we would sit down as they sat; and they would tell us stories. There was always much affection; they put their arms around us and sitting close to them, be sitting around, aunts would reach over and get us and set us on their laps. And things like that. There was always love.

I went into this school, seven years old, my folks left me there—of course, you had to go to school, so this is where they put us. And I will remember the first night I spent, I'll never forget it as long as I live. There was nobody to say good night to me. We got in line, they lined us up and took us upstairs and put us to bed ind turned out the lights, and nobody said good night to us or anything. And I remember I cried all night. And oh, I was never so lonesome, and although there were probably two hundred children there in the same dormitory with me, I felt like I was all alone. I didn't have anybody to turn to or anything. Well, the next day, we went to school. We went to church the first thing, got up real early in the morning, went to church; and I looked for my brother. I thought if I could just see him, maybe, but I couldn't even find him amongst all those boys. Well, I just kind of went on for a while, and I finally got over it. And then I had two aunts that were going to school there. And, of course, they tried in their way to mother me, but they were lonesome too, and I was lonesome—we were all lonesome, I think. But anyway, gradually you build up a resistance against this thing or something. You think, "Well, I'm not lonesome any more." And you do things I don't think you actually would do. Maybe it was for attention. Sometimes I think it was for attention that I did things, to be punished. Then I knew they would recognize me or I'd get some attention. Maybe it was a licking, but still I had attention. Well, we ate pretty good. I can't say we ate good, but we ate pretty good. We had a lot of vegetable soup which tasted real good; when you're hungry, anything tastes good. And one thing I will remember to my dying day, at four o'clock we got a great big bun. It's made of light bread. Just like you make bread, but it's a great big bun. We got this at four o'clock. And everybody waited for this four o'clock time to come—just couldn't wait. And they would pass out these big buns, they'd have baskets of them, and they'd pass them out, so everybody got a bun . . . .

And we had written letters to my parents, my brother and I had, and told them that my sister was really sick and they should come, but we never heard from them, and we couldn't figure out why my mother didn't come. Well, after we grew up we found out that they censored the mail, and anything that was said against the school, like if anybody was sick or anything, they never mailed them. And this same thing happened my last year there. My cousin got sick and died there too, at Holy Rosary, and his parents never knew until after he passed away that he was sick.

My folks finally left the reservation after my sister passed away; they decided to leave the reservation. I don't really know why. I've heard different reasons why we left the reservation. And we were put in school up here at the Rapid City Indian school. Well, we thought that this was just wonderful compared to the mission. The sisters at the mission were these old German nuns from Germany, and they didn't understand the Indian people and everything was done by force. If you didn't do this, you didn't do that, you were punished. Everything was sin. If you looked at a boy it was a sin.

Nathan Taylor

Sioux

Prairie Island Indian Community, Minnesota
Interviewed by Herbert T. Hoover
June 23, 1970

———————

Mr. Taylor was fifty-seven years old at the time of this interview.

———————

NATHAN TAYLOR My dad's name was Joseph C. Taylor. We lived in town all the time. My dad was a minister. He preached in western South Dakota, in the Black Hills, and through there. I was born at Pipestone, Minnesota. I went to town school in Pipestone, and then at the Indian school in Pipestone. My folks had five acres of land below the Indian school at Flandreau, so we moved back there one year. I went to school in town school there, and also in the Indian school. I was trying to be an auto mechanic, but I didn't get too far with it. My dad died when I was going on eighteen, so I had to get out and paddle my own canoe. I was carpentering, too— carpenter work, cement work, and stuff like that. I went through part of the tenth grade, and I quit then.

I was drafted out of Pipestone. I served here and there, the same as the rest, in World War II. I only put in twenty-seven months and twenty-two days in the service. I was a military policeman on trains from Omaha to Denver.

My dad used to make what you call genuine Indian peacepipes. You don't see very many of them any more. After my dad was gone, I took his tools and started making them. So I was the oldest peacepipe-maker still living. We had trading posts there in Pipestone, one called the Rose Trading Post. We used to sell there. I also used to camp out there in the park. It's a park there at Pipestone now. That's where I used to put up a tipi and sell my things. And while I was working at the Indian school there, my wife used to take care of that during the day.

I did a lot of digging there. It's nice to dig stones at Pipestone in the fall of the year, and all through the spring. Years ago, they used to have a ceremony. The old Indians, before they would dig stone, they would have a little ceremony—burn a little tobacco here and there. And the seams and the cracks, it would be easier for them to open it up. I believe in that. Like if you are a good man, if you are not mean. If you are mean, that pipestone will not turn out good for you. It will crack up and there will be a lot of seams.

I've been around here since the spring of 1946. I used to work in town for a construction outfit. I laid block in those days and did cement finishing. And then I've done a lot of rough carpentering. I worked for a bridge outfit. And I quit there, and worked at Hastings, two miles north of Hastings, for a nursery there, for nine years. That's where I went blind, and I quit there. On construction the highest wages were ninety-five cents an hour. At the nursery I was doing pretty good. I got a raise every year. I got up to a dollar and ninety-five.

I have four boys living, and two girls living. They are all here. One is in Hastings now, working there. The rest work over here at the [Northern States Nuclear Power] Plant, on construction. I have a son going to Central High in Red Wing.

Dorothy Lunderman

Brule Sioux

Rosebud, South Dakota
Interviewed by Joseph H. Cash
Summer 1968

Mrs. Lunderman was forty-six years old at the time of this interview.

DOROTHY LUNDERMAN   The give-away was held in honor of my oldest boy, Hubert Dillon, who went into the Army and was overseas for eighteen months and when he returned to show our thanks that he came home safely and had served his country well. My mother and I put on a big Indian dance at Rosebud Park in May of 1956. We saved our money for two years that he was in the service, and we made quilts, and we had people make things for us, and we bought other things to go along with it that we could give away. And altogether, we gave away twenty-five completely quilted star-quilts, plus over a hundred quilt tops and a lot of fancy work, such as crocheted pillow cases and dresser scarves and things. My stepfather gave, well, about $110 to $120 in cash to honor Hubert and to show his thankfulness that he had come home safely. We expected to feed over fifty people, and we ended up serving 682 people for dinner. They had a dance afterwards, which about forty dancers participated in, and we had a very large crowd there watching. Tourists from Germany, England, and France took part in the meal with us.

We were very fortunate that the people that did the singing and loaned us their loudspeaker system and everything were very good friends of our family, and they did it for nothing. Because a lot of them had had a hand in raising my son—where we lived—in the small community of Racelander where he was raised. He lived with my mother and my stepfather when he was very small, because I was working and all the people there knew him very well so they all donated their services to that.

Hubert gave the things away himself, and gave them to the people who had befriended him. From the time he was four years old on up until the day that we gave the feast. He picked the people who had done so much for him and gave them the things that he wanted to give them.

He was the oldest son I have. He went into the service shortly after he was married, and went overseas. And when they do that, you don't know whether they are going to come back in good health or whether they are going to come home at all. He came home with his health very good and nothing happened to him. This we were very, very thankful for, and to show our thanks we gave this feast. We do this because we are proud what our boys are doing and like I said, because we are very thankful that they come back to us. The Indian people like to give. They enjoy giving to someone else and making someone else happy in sharing what you have rather than to keep it all for yourself. They are very generous to each other. They will take in orphan children that don't have anyplace to go and have nothing to eat—they will feed them regardless of how little they have themselves.

I have not yet completely gotten back to where I was before, because I have given away practically every nice thing I have. So I am trying to accumulate again and I still don't have a few of the things that I gave away. But I don't feel bad about it, because they're really not that important. If I get them that's all right, and if I don't that's all right, too.

They honor their dead by remembering them—by giving away everything. Usually it is the things that the person owned personally that are given away first. Then they give away whatever they choose to give away. They will save and make quilt tops and save their money and buy little extra things, maybe handkerchiefs and clocks and things like that. And they give all this away.

JOSEPH H. CASH   Do you need a special occasion for give-aways?

A   Some will do it when their children graduate from high school, because in the past this was something which did not happen often. And nowadays, they have children that go to school through high school, and to show their thanks and appreciation that the children have had this chance to get this much education, they will give away. Or if someone has gone into the service—especially during the time of war—and they have come back safely, then they will give practically everything away that they own. Or at a funeral, then they will do it.

Some people will give away everything they own. And a lot of the women that have long hair will cut their hair very short during a mourning period. They will do that. Now, I really don't know why they cut their hair, but they do. At a time of death, many of these Indian women who have long hair will cut it real short, and until it grows out again, they are considered to be in mourning.

Purcell Rainwater

Brule Sioux

Milk's Camp, Rosebud Reservation, South Dakota
Interviewed by Joseph H. Cash
Summer 1968

———

Mr. Rainwater was in his sixties when interviewed and had long
been a renowned baseball pitcher in the area. The interviewer
had taken several futile swipes at his good curve when both were
younger.

———

JOSEPH H. CASH Purcell, you were one of the great baseball players
down here. How was that team you were on supported?

PURCELL RAINWATER Well, at that time most of us we had to supply—
we furnished our own equipment. We had a ball team in here for about six
or seven years. We had a fairly good ball club. And we won quite a few
games. Of course, we played together for a number of years, you know, and
we thought we were pretty good. Which we were. We played some pretty
good baseball teams. We had, you know, we thought we were a little bit
extra good that time. There's a lot of games we wanted to play but I don't
know, for some reason they didn't want to play us.

Q Well, when you travel to play games do you have to pay for it all
yourself?

A Yes, we always all try to help pay for our own expenses traveling
back and forth.

Q Do they still have a team down here?

A No, they don't have a ball team any more. Seems like the young
fellows for some reason or another never—I don't know—just don't care for
baseball. I played ball across the river one year, and I think we had eleven
men on the team. And they only had one player from this town, and he
never got a chance to play at all during the summer. And the rest of us, we

were all from different parts of the country. You know, they picked them out here and there from all over the country.

Q And they paid you?

A Yes, we got paid. And of course, we were pretty good. I think the only team that beat us that year was Sioux City. They beat us. Of course, they had a western league team. And of course, our manager got us the game. We had a celebration in town there. When the ball club pulled in, it was the Sioux City Stockyards. So they beat us. Of course, they didn't beat us too bad. I think they beat us only two or three runs. Then we played a bunch from Texas, a traveling club. I think we beat them two and three. A western league outfit going through the country at that time, traveling club. After the game the manager called us up to his room and he asked us if two of us, if we'd like to have a better chance of playing a higher league ball. A little higher up. And I told him I would. He asked me if I would be able to go down to Texas the following spring. But when the time came, you know, that was during the hard years, and I didn't even have the money to get out of the county, let alone going way down there. The other boy was named Joe Cook; he's from down Wagner, from Greenwood Reservation. So we didn't get to go. Other than that, I would have went to Texas and joined the western league down there. We just didn't have the money to get out of the county.

Jake Herman

Brule Sioux

Pine Ridge Reservation, South Dakota
Interviewed by Joseph H. Cash
Summer 1967

Jake Herman was one of America's most famed rodeo clowns. A
Brule Sioux, he married an Oglala girl and was elected as a
member of the Oglala tribal council. He ran his own museum,
painted pictures, made artifacts, and talked endlessly about tribal
history before his death in 1970. He was in his eighties at the
time of this interview.

JOSEPH H. CASH   How did you get started in this business of being
a rodeo clown, Jake?

JAKE HERMAN   Well, I went to Carlisle and played football and basket-
ball there.

Q   That was after Jim Thorpe was there, wasn't it?

A   After Thorpe was there. Then Thorpe was going to organize a
team at Altoona. His manager wanted me down there, and I was going to
play in it, you know, at that time it was new. I went down there. I happened to go to a wild west show, I broke horses, and I'd trick ride out here
the western way. And I went there, and I joined the show and I went down
south. I never did meet up with Thorpe. I played shows for two years. I
watched those other clowns.

Q   Whose show was it?

A   Jack King's Wild West Show and Rodel Royal Circus. They had a
wild west concert, and then I traveled with Reuben and Cherry—Colonel
McNabe. I worked for different ones. I found out the best way to be a
clown. Well, the rodeo clown's got to have his, all his material, like mule or
skunk or dog; and he must be able to ride and rope. And I do all them
things, but I took advantage of the advantage. And then as a comedy actor.

And I came back here and I did a little clowning and finally I made up my mind that's one way of making money, so I started out. I wasn't any big-time clown, but I clowned quite a few shows in my days.

Q When did you quit?

A I quit in '43. I was up in age then, I was about fifty, and I couldn't fight those bulls out. I lost my pep, and I barely got out of the way, and I thought before I got killed I better quit. And I couldn't stay on them, you know, I'd get throwed off. I never was crippled, but it got pretty rough.

Noah White

Winnebago

Prairie Island Indian Community, Minnesota
Interviewed by Herbert T. Hoover
June 25, 1970

———————

Mr. White, the only member of the Winnebago tribe at Prairie
Island, is a skilled craftsman, an excellent dancer, and a leader
in the Native American Church. He was fifty-three years old at
the time of this interview.

———————

NOAH WHITE   My Indian name, interpreted into English, would mean
something similar to Whirlwind Thunder. I am from the Winnebago tribe,
a fullblood Indian. I am a descendant of two different clanships—the Thunder Clan and Buffalo Clan. As far as my education goes, I went to a
Government boarding school in Genoa, Nebraska. I spent twelve years
there. And after that I had one year of a commercial course in Pierre, South
Dakota. Then I went back to the reservation for a couple of years. From
there on, I just went out to seek jobs wherever I could find employment,
and returned to the reservation when I was unemployed. Then, in the early
forties, I went into the service and was there until the latter part of 1945.

I went into school without being able to talk English at all, so they
had to have an interpreter from my own tribe to interpret for me for the
first year or so, until I began to learn the English language. After that, we
were forbidden to speak our own language. We were taught to forget our
culture and learn everything we could about the white man's ways. That
was in the twenties and up to the middle thirties.

Commissioner Collier had some of that changed, so in some Indian
schools we would be able to send for our Indian costumes and hold tribal
dances during commencement week. It didn't last too long, because the
school closed up. But in most of the schools today, they are trying to revive
all of the traditions of the various tribes. They are trying to teach basket

weaving and beadwork. They are trying to teach tribal dances and tribal singing. And in some places they even teach the language. The various Indian tribes are trying to bring back their own languages. There are quite a few of them that have lost their language, however.

At Genoa school, I had mostly academics just like any other high school—history, science, and anything pertaining to academics. For half of the day the boys that were from the seventh grade on up had to work in order to help in maintaining the school. We could learn any kind of vocation that we wanted to learn. They didn't have welders then; they used to call it blacksmithing. And you could learn crop farming, or poultry. Or you could learn truck farming. And they had a hog farm there; they had a dairy farm. Just about anything—you could go into music or carpentry. They had a baking school there—anything that the individual wanted to learn, they could pick up.

They marched on the same basis as a military school. It was nothing to see children five years old learning how to drill like they do in the services today. For the larger boys they had smaller dormitories. They had regular officers just like they do in the service. The officers slept two or three to a room, four to a room. But the other students slept in large dormitories where there were sometimes ten, fifteen to a dormitory. Some even maybe about twenty in a dormitory. The smaller boys all lived in large dormitories, in larger rooms. The only ones that had small rooms were the officers. They had a captain for each company; and they had majors. That ran along the same line in our girls' dormitories. They had the same thing.

Some got home every summer to see their parents, and everything. But I was one of the unfortunate ones. I didn't get a chance to go home at all for thirteen years . . . . One thing nice I found out about a Government school is you learned discipline. If nothing else, you disciplined yourself. You can tell the students that went to a Government school, and the ones that didn't.

Lawrence Gingway

Ottawa

Crow Creek Reservation, South Dakota
Interviewed by Joseph H. Cash
Summer 1968

Mr. Gingway is married to a Yanktonais Sioux and has owned
and operated a grocery and meat market on the reservation for a
number of years. He was fifty-four years old at the time of this
interview.

LAWRENCE GINGWAY   We have a little trouble getting rid of our T-bone
steaks because the people really aren't used to eating a good cut of meat,
although they're changing their ways now and buying a little bit better
grade of meat than they used to. We used to cut up all our T-bones, or
practically all our steaks, for boiling beef because that's all they knew how
to cook or how to prepare; but now, since the new generation is coming on,
I would say that they learned to prepare their meat a little different.

JOSEPH H. CASH   What about the variety meats—liver, kidneys, tripe?

A   They still ask for tripe and scraps and one thing or another, but I
think it's because they are a little short of money at the time. I don't think
it's a matter of preference.

The biggest food item is meat. They don't care too much for canned
stuff, although they do go for fresh fruit when we have it. But their biggest item is meat. If you get a good grade of meat, good cut of meat for
them, they'll buy it.

Q   Do they still eat any of the native foods like the Indian turnips or
berries, that sort of thing?

A   Yes, if we can get them, they still use them. They're not as ambitious, shall we say, as they used to be. They used to go out and pick these
things and save them for the winter, but they don't do that any more.
Maybe it's because of the transportation problem, but they don't seem to

do it anyway. But they will eat it if they can get it and prepare it.

Q Is that just the older generation?

A Well, some of the younger ones are still using it, but not too many. It's more the older generation. They still make the fried bread.

Q Does anybody around here make pemmican?

A Yes, they call it *wasna*. Yes, I think that is what they call it here. Well, there again, I think it's the same problem. They don't get the ingredients to make it, although I think they would eat it if they had material to make it with.

Q At celebrations or special occasions, do they make any attempt to eat Indian foods?

A Oh, not too much, although they do prepare some like their fried bread, serve it along with their soup or whatever they've got. It's usually boiled meat. They buy a lot of bread from us, a matter of fact. They buy quite a little more than they should really, because of their commodity flour that they get, you know. They should use that, but they buy a real lot of bread. I am not hollering about that, it's a good thing, but they really have a lot of flour that they should use up.

Q Indians seem to like things that are sweet.

A I think the older generation maybe might on account of their greasy meat; their buffalo, I imagine was pretty greasy, and they used the whole thing. Now they use this kidney fat. They usually try to get some from us—the kidney fat—and they render that and eat it like butter. That's just the same as bone marrow—they eat bone marrow raw. They get a T-bone steak and they'll take that bone marrow out and eat it raw. It's good—you ought to try it.

Father Vine Deloria

Sioux

Vermillion, South Dakota
Interviewed by Herbert T. Hoover
November 30, 1970

Father Deloria enjoys great respect among both Indians and non-Indians across the Middle West as a clergyman and moral leader. An Episcopal priest for several decades, he was in his sixties and rector of St. Paul's Episcopal Church at Vermillion, when interviewed.

FATHER DELORIA   When I first left the Standing Rock Reservation and went off to school, and would go back, I was too young to understand things were changing rapidly.

I left the reservation in 1916, and only about ten years before that they forced allotment on us. The Indians had owned the whole of Standing Rock Reservation tribally, so that you could live anywhere you wanted. And just about everybody was interested in two things—horses and cattle. Buffalos were gone. But they had always been interested—at least for four hundred years—in horses. Coronado left some here, and they got more. They always had had buffalo. So stock-raising industry was right up their alley. And so they got along with minimal governmental supervision. There were lots of Indian police, more to keep Indians in than whites out. They patrolled on horseback along the fence all the time. Perhaps people felt sorry for us for being in there. But to me those were the happiest days in my life. Just get on a horse and go in any direction. You never ran into a fence. There would be a little fence, a small piece like twenty acres where a man lived, and had just a little pasture to keep a horse or two to look for his stock.

The Government did some good things, like blacksmithing and carpentry and cobblers, and so on. They taught the Indians. They were pushing them on what I would call rural economy. And they knew how. Of course, they knew already nobody could beat them on drying meat. They cut it thin, sun-dried it, and it rarely spoiled. They could get from the ground corn, squash, beans—all staple foods. They lived that way for a long time.

Well, I left there. I remembered what those people were like. I was away for fifteen years, actually from 1916 to 1931 . . . . I came back and saw the Pine Ridge Indians, and I was shocked at how they had changed physically, mentally, morally, spiritually, socially, and economically, from what I had known. I thought it was just the Pine Ridge, so I said, "Well, I will go back for a visit with the Standing Rock." I went back there, and it was the same. Here they had taken the fences down, and they had all kinds of white people in there. I don't want to criticize anybody, but for some reason they had a bad effect on the Indians—who were not the people I left.

When I left, those Indians on the Standing Rock, the Sioux, [they were] like Columbus said—gentle beings, souls of hospitality, serious and happy, faithful and trustful, walking in beauty, and in possession of a spiritual religion. Like Catlin said, without ever hearing the Bible they live it. And the Ten Commandments—they never used lock and key. They never stole a thing . . . .

And then I was gone about nine years again. And I came back, and my golly, there was change. Broken families, drinking, idleness. They lost incentive for living. They just didn't care. And the greatest thing they were losing was religion. You know what I think? When the Christian religion first went among the Dakotas, they took to it, and they made a great church out of it. The Roman Catholic, Episcopalian, Congregational—they all were terrific churches. Why? Because Christianity ran itself into a people who already, in their own right, were of spiritual nature. But during the past one hundred years they had been going on their reserve—their spiritual stockpile. So they were spiritually degraded.

Then, of course, there was a physical side. The Government, unfortunately, thought they knew what was good for the Indians.

Depression, war, and a revival of self-government

Cato Valandra

Long-time Rosebud tribal chairman, Cato Valandra is an enterprising businessman.

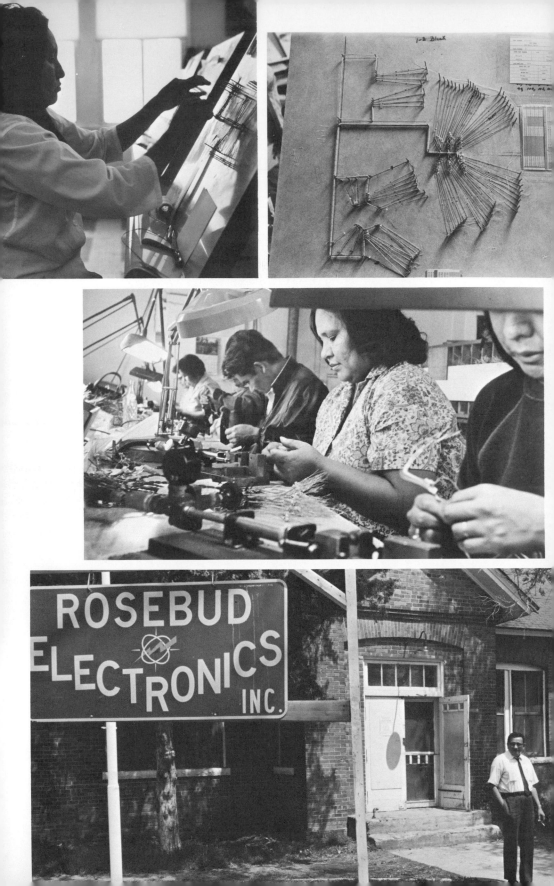

Mr. Valandra's largest business, Rosebud Electronics Co., started in 1967 with three people. Now 90 employees wind complex wired circuits. To promote business interest in Rosebud, he tested workers in an electronics firm in St. Cloud, Minnesota, against the Indians on the reservation for concentration span, attention to detail, and such qualities. The Indians proved more competent for this type of work than non-Indians.

Lakota Arts, another Valandra enterprise, reproduces high quality prints of American classics by means of a special printing process. Charles Russell's Western scenes are in frequent demand. Mr. Valandra discusses progress with the plant manager (top).

As secretary-treasurer of Rosebud Housing Authority, Mr. Valandra inspects a burned-out house. He queries the Todd County extension agent about the shortage of jobs available for Indians.

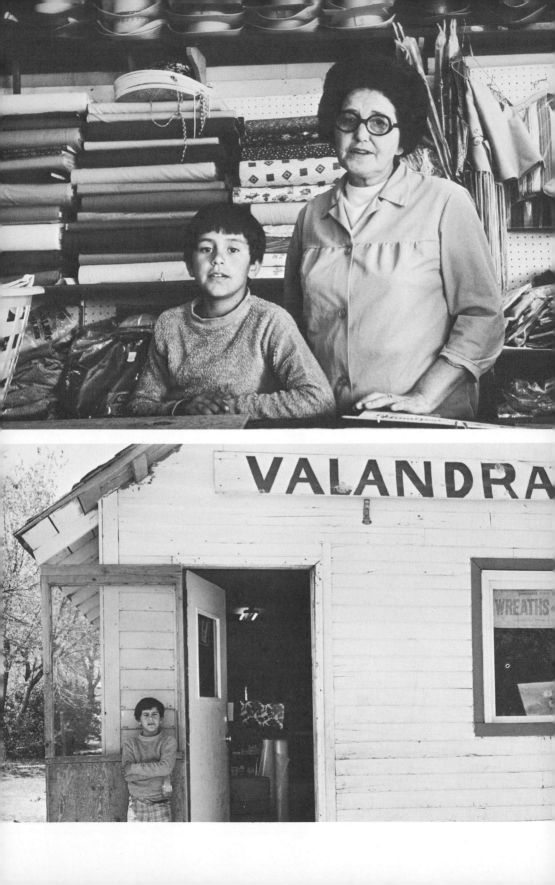

Mrs. Valandra and part-time helper Lee Valandra manage the Valandra grocery and variety store in St. Francis (opposite). Judy Valandra studies world geography at school (above). Howard Valandra runs one of the family service stations (right).

Mr. Valandra's sons and their friends play on the front porch of the Valandra home in Rosebud (below).

Ben Reifel

Brule Sioux

Washington, D.C.
Interviewed by Joseph H. Cash
Summer 1967

Ben Reifel has a long and distinguished career. A long-time
Bureau of Indian Affairs executive, he has a Ph.D. from Harvard
and was a United States representative from South Dakota's First
Congressional District at the time he was interviewed.

JOSEPH H. CASH   Congressman, you were very active in the thirties on
these Rosebud and Pine Ridge Reservations in connection with this Indian
Reorganization Act, were you not?

BEN REIFEL   I was a farm agent at Oglala, South Dakota, on the Pine
Ridge Reservation in 1933. When the bill was being considered by the
Indians on the reservations and regional conferences, at the same time it
was being considered here in the Congress prior to enactment, I was im-
pressed with the possibilities of the bill. The original plan was to set up a
well-coordinated system of government by tribes. One of the primary benefits that I thought would come from it would be that if they did go through
with their judicial system, whereby the tribal courts tied in with the federal system of courts, this would then correct the weakness in Indian courts
where there is no appeal for the tribal organization or for the tribal courts.
And that, of course, persists to the present time and is one of the weak-
nesses in the judicial system of tribal courts. Now they're attempting to correct this. Well, there were many aspects of the original plan written out in
the bill that was presented to Congress that got changed. I think it was a
plan for communal use of the tribal property and in the development of the
property on a communal basis. I think in the minds of some, this was identi-
fied with communism in some way or another, when really it was nothing
more than enlarging on present tribal holdings of especially land in common. That is the case today on many of the reservations—certain areas of

121

land that are held in tribal ownership which is held in common. And it was thought to develop these programs, these properties, on a communal basis. One of the major defects in the proposal, I think, at least as far as the members of Congress were concerned at that time, was divesting an individual of his property without his consent. Some of the provisions of the proposal would take land that was alloted in severalty to an individual and put it back into common ownership. And this was believed to be in violation of personal property rights without due recourse to the courts. So it finally came out in a much modified program known as the Wheeler-Howard Act and subsequently designated as the Indian Reorganization Act of 1934. Well, I happened to be on the Pine Ridge Reservation, as I said, as a farm agent. I could speak and write the Sioux language and took one of those old A-B-C charts that they used to use in the Indian schools on the little stand. And on one side I would write a little synopsis of each section —I think there were some eighteen sections to the law—and then right alongside of it I would put the Indian translation and draw some pictures to illustrate what it meant. I did this in my farm district. And when the tribal leaders met in reservation-wide meetings, they were having it explained to them, but the people from the district in which I was working attending the meeting seemed to be better informed. Others wanted to know where they got the information. So I was down there helping with it. The superintendent of the reservation at that time, James H. McGregor, sent word out to me to come up and put on my chalk-talk for the tribal leaders. And I went with him from one district on the reservation to another, explaining the law.

Q   Were you hired to do this?

A   I was a farm agent. Of course the superintendent—a federal employee on the Pine Ridge Reservation—the superintendent had authority to delegate the employees to other assignments other than their primary assignment for short periods of time. So I was with the superintendent at the meetings on the reservations. There was considerable agitation against the legislation because the older members of the tribe—and some of the younger ones, too—felt that the lands were going to be taken away from them and put into common ownership. They were very fearful of this. I didn't blame them for this, and I think this was a carry-over from the original provisions of the bill, or rather the original bill that was proposed by John Collier who was then Commissioner of Indian Affairs. He had held regional meetings where the tribes would come in, and he was trying to develop a perceptivity on the part of the Indians for the legislation.

They had one in Rapid City. I remember I attended that one. Back in those days I was first in the Government service. But I became very interested, so I took annual leave and went up there. I spent all of the time on the conferences listening to what was going on. Well, there was this opposition then to the bill itself. Now the act was unusual in that unless the

Indians turned it down it would go into effect. It would have a referendum on it. So the law was passed by Congress subject to the acceptance/rejection by the tribe. This made it necessary to go out and explain to the tribes prior to the elections to be held, the provisions of the act. And so, with the little experience that I had on the reservations explaining with my charts, Joe Jennings—who was Superintendent of Indian Education for South Dakota —was designated by the Commissioner of Indian Affairs to take responsibility for explaining the Indian Reorganization Act to tribes throughout South Dakota, Montana, Nebraska, and North Dakota. Being aware of what I was doing at Pine Ridge, he asked the superintendent if I could be used to do this explanation with him in the Sioux country because I spoke the Sioux language. So I traveled throughout the state of South Dakota to the various Indian tribes that were scheduled to vote on the legislation and explained these provisions. And following that, some tribes adopted and some did not. I remember Crow Creek was one tribe that turned it down. Sisseton was another. And I think they turned the legislation down completely. And I believe also the Yankton Reservation. And by this time, July of 1935, the Commissioner established under the law some field agents to help with the promotion of the legislation on Indian reservations. I was designated as one of the first to be a field agent. In July of 1935 I got the appointment and then I came down to Washington in March of that year and was down here a couple of months getting some background information on it. Then I was headquartered in Pierre after that. And I was in Pierre until 1942 when the war broke out and then I was ordered to active duty. But during that seven-year period I worked with Indian tribes explaining these provisions of the law, and when they got that done, then the tribes—if they wanted to move ahead—had to adopt the constitution and bylaws. Following that, they could establish a corporate charter. All of these had to be explained to the tribal members, then voted upon, in an open election. They got a great deal of opposition and much excitement for it. A group of camps developed for it, one against the other. And in the Dakotas, we had what was a group called the old dealers. You see, this emerged out of the Roosevelt New Deal period and so Collier, the Commissioner, said that we'd have a new deal for the Indians. And so this was dubbed the new deal. And anyone who was for it was a new dealer, and the older members felt themselves losing control. At Pine Ridge, they had seven districts on the reservation. On each of the seven districts, I think they had ten delegates who would come to a tribal council, and they'd sit there and carry on for three or four days. This would be eighty or ninety people coming together. This was a kind of traditional system where they didn't have any power at all, but they did have an opportunity to express their views and give vent to some of their feelings. I think they saw themselves losing this, whatever influence they had. At least their participation in the Indian system.

Q Do you think it was an old generation of leadership opposing a new?

A It was the old generation of leadership opposing it. And to this day you have this older group. I think they still look upon themselves as the so-called old dealers. The new dealers they call *Tey-cha*, meaning the new way of life. And then they have the old-timers.

Q Did you notice in the opposition any difference between the mixed bloods and the full bloods?

A Yes. Well, of course, you had the old-timers, the older people were largely full bloods. And then you had among them opportunists who tended to help the older ones and could not see themselves getting into the new system. Either by lack of education or because of their prior lack of leadership, they were in a position because they could speak English and could identify themselves and provide a means of communication on the part of the so-called old dealers against the new program.

Another problem we had with it, and still have with the Indian administration, is that so many things are the land and property of the tribe and held in the name of the United States in trust. And the Congress charged the Secretary of Interior with the responsibility of exercising that trust. Therefore, over the years, as certain rules and regulations were established for the protection or exercise of that trust, every ·honest effort I think, was designed to protect the Indians in the use of their property. And so the constitution as it was written says in practically every section of it "with the approval of the Secretary of Interior," and if he doesn't turn it down within a certain period of time, it becomes effective. And the old dealers said, "Well, I told you. The Secretary of Interior is still going to have control. He's having control. You've got to go to him." The newer ones said, of course, that this was necessary under the circumstances, but at some point when they tried to move beyond what the law would permit, the secretary would step in to prevent its completion of the enactment being carried in force. Then they would begin to get shaken a bit, feeling that they were unnecessarily restrained. There were provisions in the constitution by which after a certain period the secretary's authority would expire. But never was there any authority in the constitution where the secretary's trust over responsibility was completely taken away. It couldn't be, because if the Indians were to keep their land in trust subject to or not subject to local taxation, then it would have to be considered—at least in a sense—a kind of federal property because it would be in the name of the United States, being held in trust. There was this feeling that the tribal council did not get enough authority to really do the things they wanted to do on behalf of the people they represented. Along with it, we also had this federal charter of the corporation. And that again created a lot of difficulty for the old-timers because the charter authorized the tribe to accept gifts and property, and also to hypothecate tribal property for any loans that they may get from the Federal Government. The older people, those who were opposed, said, "Well, here's a group of people that are governing our people. They are a small group; they aren't representing all the people." And the older people didn't think they were being represented adequately. So a great deal of feeling about the acceptance of the charter was that this would cause them to lose the land. And if they borrowed the money, the Federal Government would come along later on, and if they want to claim this would be an offset against the claim. There are many things like that— every kind of ghost was raised against it that they could imagine. And some of it had just enough fact to it to give it a color of truth. And I could understand their apprehensiveness on this regard.

The law was accepted at Pine Ridge, but they didn't take the corporate charter. At Rosebud, I guess they took all three; I think that probably was true. Lower Brule accepted all three. Crow Creek didn't accept anything. Standing Rock accepted the law, but never got a constitution or a charter. Cheyenne River accepted all three as I recall.

Q   The New Deal did a lot of other things as well as the Indian Reorganization Act. I've heard a lot of people say it pushed education on the reservations. At that time an Indian on the reservation would not get through high school, for example.

A   Mr. Collier had the feeling, and I've heard him say that the Indians are in the vanguard of this world-wide loop back into the land. And they set up similar rehabilitation projects and canning kitchens and little cottages around, and developed little irrigation plots on Red Shirt Table in Pine Ridge—local turkey, poultry projects, cattle projects, and things that seemingly went great guns. They established a school there. It was really a community school. The teacher and his wife and his whole family lived and worked with this group. It was quite an exciting sort of thing if this was really happening. But World War II came along and the industrial revolution really came into its own. In agriculture, we were able to produce more than we were able to before, even with half the young farmers off the land . . . .

I think 1928 really set the basis for improvement in education. Up until then, there wasn't much done in the boarding school. There was no home demonstration agent. There were no home economics teachers in the schools that were qualified as they are required to be qualified under the Smith-Hughes and other programs. About 1928, and with the Meriam survey, it began to bring in professionally qualified people—more doctors, more nurses, more teachers—and the New Deal sort of built right on this. One of the misfortunes among the Indians, I feel personally, was the part where education was concerned. That the cause of this whole national feeling of reversion to the land, and that the Indians were in the vanguard, leadership in the Indian education was . . . well, the first Director of Indian Education in the Bureau of Indian Affairs in the New Deal—I can't think of his name right at this moment—was the first president from the National Progressive Education Association. And he wanted to move in on "learning by doing" and this was even carried further by the second president of the National Progressive Education Association. I myself think a little bit of education and training and think there's nothing wrong with the John Dewey approach if you have enough well-trained teachers and the facilities and equipment to follow the John Dewey method. But here we had an educator come out—Dr. Willard Beatty—and he said, "Throw out the curriculum, throw out the stated courses. Study and you won't find any books in the classroom." And these poor teachers were just going around because they've never been taught how to handle the situation. A few conferences were held and wonderful speeches were made about the value of the Dewey approach and progressive education. And so he had kids roaming around trying to find something to do. And through that period, I think that a lot of time was lost. There was a feeling—the Indians went away to boarding schools and they came back to the reservations anyway, so why train them to leave? Why not train them to stay where they are? So you had goats brought in, little projects where the little kids would work with chickens or rabbits and gardens, and they tended to be losing sight of learning to read and write and to figure. Then they said, "You could learn these things just as rapidly if you related your arithmetic to the chicken house and goats, how much milk a goat had and all that." But the teachers just weren't prepared for this. And as a consequence, I think they lost lots of time there. But there was a part of the Meriam survey and a start in the direction of improving the educational system back in 1928. This was carried through so you got some better school buildings, for instance. And then, of course, with the Second World War coming along, you apparently had a lot of young people going in for the armed forces. You have the Navajos, for instance, who had a real awakening for the need of education. And so they were able to get the Navajos to bring their children to school. But other than the general revival of bringing additional money for facilities, I think the methods that were implemented—as a result of this wave of progressive education sweeping the country—I don't believe it did the Indian education system much help, as far as the Indian children are concerned. There was, of course, out of the Indian Reorganization Act, a step up in the educational loan programs that were being made available to Indians. But this was also started back in 1928. In 1928, I got one of the first loans made available under the Indian program as recommended by the Meriam survey, where an Indian could borrow money and not have to pay any interest until he got a job or he got out. And over a period of four years at Brookings, from 1928 to 1932, I borrowed $900. So whatever was done in education, or anything in Indian affairs, was really kind of a foundation established as a result of the recommendation of the Meriam survey.

Q How do you think the law and order system worked under the Wheeler-Howard Act?

A Well, up until the time of the Wheeler-Howard Act, of course, you just had the tribal courts. And there really wasn't too much necessity for a sophisticated court system. You had one of the old tribal leaders who was respected in the community, and he was designated by the superintendent of the reservation as the judge. And you had some tribal policemen. And then there was a court, and a code of tribal offenses set up—blanket for the United States I guess. And if the Indian violated this, then he was brought before the tribal judge. And the judge—probably one who couldn't read or write—issued a sentence to him, and that's about all there was.

There was an effort made, as I say, under the original bill to set up a real sophisticated federal court system that would go all the way from the little tribal community right up to federal court if necessary, and have it appealed just like any other. But in the revising and amending of the bill, it came out there wasn't any federal court set up. So all they had then was for the tribal constitution to provide. The law said whatever laws, whatever powers the Indian tribe had, was not taken away from them by the Government; the tribe still had them. And one of these was law and order jurisdiction over its people. On the basis that the constitution provided that the tribal council was to establish a law and order code for the reservation. And then they brought in the state codes, in most instances along with the federal laws, in trying to work out the best compromise to fit the situation on the reservation. And so you actually had a code of offenses defining what an offense was, and they also laid the limits down as to what the sentence would be. And then there was a provision in it that the individual would be informed of his rights and all of this sort of thing.

But again, because the courts couldn't pay very much, a person who would accept the responsibilities of tribal judge was usually somebody who, if he had a high school education, was fortunate. In most instances, he probably had not much better than an eighth-grade education. This was probably not too bad; I mean, if he had good judgment and ability. But the weakness of the whole system was—and still is—that this court, once it finds an individual guilty, there is no appeal from it. I mean, this is it. He can't appeal it. And we're still worrying with it. There was nothing in the Indian Reorganization Act that enabled a case to be carried beyond—the tribe is the final authority. And in a small community like Pine Ridge, there are a lot of painful experiences that result when a person gets thrown in jail and there's no appeal on it. But there has not been any way to rectify it. Now, as I say, the original bill—had it gone through—would have set up a system of district Indian courts under the federal system. It had a circuit court you could appeal right up to the Supreme Court if necessary. But now on the reservations you have the state law applying in certain instances, the federal law applying in certain instances; and then there's this no-man's land, so to speak, in which the tribal courts apply, and it is in this area that the tribal member is sometimes without any recourse to appeal.

Q   Do you think the Indians are better off under the Indian Reorganization Act than the previous system?

A   Oh, yes. I think the educational consequences under the Indian Reorganization Act in constitutional government for instance—all the discussions that have gone on as to one's rights with respect to laws. These are the things that have never been discussed to any extent before. The people directly involved with the federal law without being considered by Congress. It was being talked over with them before enactment of the law. And then they talked about it all the time it was in Congress and they sent delegations down. And following that they had an opportunity to reconsider whether they wanted the law or not. And then after that, after they accept the law, or go through all the problems of setting up the constitution and bylaws, and then adopting, formulating resolutions and ordinances, and all of this, I think it was helpful for improving their knowledge of government and our society generally. I think it is kind of confusing—when you've got an Indian on the reservation, there's more laws applying to him than the average citizen in the country.

Q   Do you think he's better off economically under the Wheeler-Howard Act?

A   Yes. In many respects the Wheeler-Howard Act made possible these loans that are still being expanded in amounts. Authorizations are increasing. That made the loans to the individuals at a lower rate of interest than he could get through the Farmers Home Administration. The problem there again is here is a person who gets a loan and his neighbor may feel that he's just as qualified as the fellow who got the loan. Then you build up some neighborhood jealousy as a result of that. You can't get enough money to take care of everybody so you've got to be selective. You select those who could benefit most rapidly from this. In many instances, it would be individuals just a little above the margin. And this makes the other fellow say, "Why can't I?" Or the tribal council or the credit board is helping relatives, for all kinds of reasons. So you disappoint more people than you help. I think it's true today—our efforts to try and help the poor really get into some massive problems. And you touch a little here and a little there, and you actually sometimes raise hopes of people beyond possibilities of meeting them. And with these programs, I think it would happen on any reservation. But on the balance, they've got more loans out that have helped more people from this standpoint. They have improved the law and order system so that the individual, in spite of everything, has a better chance.

I remember as a kid, I was in college, and I was working in a store in Rosebud. My younger brother came up and said one of my other brothers was in jail right there in the agency town. So I went over and he said he was asleep in the back room of the pool hall my father owned in the little town of Parmalee. And there was a big fuss between the pool hall and the garage. There was a big fight out there and a bunch of people got beat up and arrested. My brother was working then, helping dig a basement for a theatre there. He said the policemen came up and said, "You're under arrest," and brought him in. He said, "What for?" "Well, you were in this fight last night." So he was sitting down there in jail and I went over and I just happened to know the superintendent of the reservation, so I went over and said, "I've got my brother in jail over here." And I gave him my brother's explanation. So he wrote out a little slip, and I took it down to the policeman, and he released him. I mean, you have this sort of thing so that it's pretty much on a personal basis. I think they intended to eliminate this to some degree. I think it can still happen, but I think they intended to make the law enforcement programs a little more sophisticated in recognizing the rights of the individuals.

And all of this is, I think, on the plus side over what it was before. The land program that is being worked out in Rosebud through all the trials and tribulations it's gone through—I think that also is an improvement in the right direction. The educational loan programs that the Indian Reorganization Act increased in amount and are continuing to be increased. All these are a forerunner of what we have on reservations as a whole. There were for the Sioux country—particularly at Pine Ridge, Cheyenne River, for instance, even up to the present time—the old provisions called Sioux benefits. If an Indian had an allotment of land and was living at the age of eighteen, he was entitled to some money. Initially, when an Indian under the Allotment Act of 1887 or 1889 . . . for instance, my mother got her allotment—when she became eighteen she got a team of horses, three milk cows, a rake, a hoe, a harrow, a wagon, kettles, and a whole bunch of stuff which was supposed to help. The idea was that this was to help them settle on this quarter section of land. Well, they soon found this to be an awkward arrangement, so they commuted the value of this to cash. And when I was in high school in Brookings, I became eighteen. I made my application, and I got somewhere in the neighborhood of $600. The commuted value of these items at that time was $600. Today the commuted value is around $1200 or $1300. So the law was written in such a way that at the time of the passage of the law, any tribe that had a lot of land that was too poor to be allotted, it required that all the tribal land that was unallotted would be added up and divided by eighty. The reason was that if the Indian couldn't have the land allotted to him then at least they ought to divide the lands up into half the amount. So then they took the figure eighty and divided all the acres. And this gave them that many so-called Sioux benefits, and they could issue them. And then, as every child became eighteen years of age, he was entitled not to an allotment of land, but to this commuted value of these Sioux benefits. So Pine Ridge up to the present time is still getting Sioux benefits. It's amounted up to several hundreds of thousands of dollars. Rosebud had a few, but not very many, because it didn't have so much tribal land. Pine Ridge had a little more, but they took these on the basis of those who were the oldest individuals and on down who didn't get allotments.

What that did was to enable a tribe like Cheyenne River to cash in on every acre on Sioux benefit. Double what it would have gotten and more, because previous to this, as soon as a child was born, the parents would go out and buy a piece of land. With the death rate being high, many of those pieces they [the parents] cashed in on Sioux benefits because the child passed away before he reached eighteen. However, this guaranteed that every eighty-acre tract, or at least every unit equivalent to eighty acres bought from the tribe, there were Sioux benefits for each of the eighty-acre tracts of tribal land that were left. So this was a side benefit; of course, that didn't apply to other tribes.

Q   What do you think needs to be done yet, Congressman?

A   Well, I think one of the things we have to do is step up our education. And do everything we can to get every kid in school and started in school as early as possible. And I hope that eventually we can get nursery schools and kindergarten, and keep these boys and girls in school right through high school. And then following high school, direct them into either vocational projects—if their aptitudes are such that this is where they should go—or into professions. This I think is essential. Most of the Indian reservations are located in areas in which they are too far from industrial areas. And they're so isolated, the possibility of bringing industry to a reservation is almost nil. And I think we have to plan on that basis. So education is important. We need to step up our educational programs, which means we're going to have to put in more money than we're putting in now. And we're going to have to help these kids coming from broken homes, orphans and half-orphans. You've got to almost work with them as parents because they don't have parents to encourage them to go on. They're going to have to have more money to fix their teeth, to buy their clothing, eyeglasses, and a lot of these things the parents provide which will be necessary, or they're going to drop out of school. We just have to continue to make welfare expenditures.

Ramon Roubideaux

Brule Sioux

Fort Pierre, South Dakota
Interviewed by Joseph H. Cash
Summer 1968

Mr. Roubideaux is an attorney, one of the finest trial lawyers in
South Dakota, and the nominee of the Democratic party for
Attorney General of South Dakota. He was forty-three years old
at the time of this interview.

RAMON ROUBIDEAUX   As far as the Indian Reorganization Act is concerned, I think this is possibly one of the best intentioned but unfortunate
happenings that could have possibly taken place as far as the Indian people
are concerned. Although it did stop the sale of Indian lands and did stop
the allotment system, it created a socialistic society and set the Indian people apart from the mainstream of American life and made them a problem.
It has substituted in place of the governing system that the Indians had
prior to the Indian Reorganization Act a white man's idea of how they
should live—rather a paternalistic type of government which has as its object
the socializing of all the activities of the Indian people. While the framers
of this act and the ones who are responsible for the idea of formulating it
probably had the best intentions in the world, I cannot help but think that
there was, maybe not an overt conspiracy, but one in the back of the mind
of these bureaucrats to really perpetuate their own existence.

When I speak of bureaucrats, I not only include the actual officeholders but the families and friends of all these officeholders who form the
controlling and guiding memberships of these eastern Indian organizations.
To make myself a little clearer, I want to elaborate a little on the effects of
the Indian Reorganization Act insofar as it has deterred the development
and the independent thinking of the Indian people. In the first place, it set
the Indian aside as a problem. The Indian was told that he was a problem

from the very day that he was born under this system, and as he grew older, by the presence of these so-called experts in agriculture and ranching and other activities they were paying lip service to teaching the Indians, he was somehow made to feel that he was inferior, that he wasn't able to compete. So that the whole system emphasized the activities of the Indians as a whole for the benefit of the whole, rather than the individual private enterprise system of our American system. He wasn't taught to be a capitalist, which he must be taught in order for him to survive in this country . . . .

Their main objective was to show what they've been doing to members of Congress on the Appropriations Committee, to justify the millions of dollars they were spending, when actually the Indian was getting little or no benefit from any of this. And I think the main thing that was wrong with the whole thing was that the setting of the Indian aside on a different place in the state, designating him as a problem, making him feel he was a problem, beating down rebels, beating down Indians who expressed any independent thinking, rewarding collaborators, rewarding them with positions of importance and completely stifling independent and creative thinking from the Indian people, having different laws apply to him, setting up a different kind of government . . . .

It's not self-government, because self-government by permission is no self-government at all. Everything that the Indian Reorganization Act brought in under the guise of self-government was subject to the approval or the concurrence of the Secretary of the Interior or his authorized representative—the superintendent. These Indians have never made policy decisions; they have never been able to use creative thinking. Everything they've done has been under the wing of the Government; it's just like the rich kid with the rich father. Everything is planned for him, he never develops this mind of his.

Alfred DuBray

Sioux

Winnebago Reservation, Nebraska
Interviewed by Herbert T. Hoover
July 28, 1970

———

Mr. DuBray has been close to developments in Indian affairs
throughout his life, as a reservation resident and as an official.
He was superintendent of the Winnebago agency and fifty-seven
years old at the time of this interview.

———

ALFRED DUBRAY I'm originally from South Dakota—was born on the
Rosebud Reservation and grew up there on the reservation until, I guess, I
was twenty years of age. I went to high school in Winner. Of course, this
was in the Depression days. When I went to college it was a rather difficult
thing. But I did manage to go to finish a course in business administration
at Mitchell—two years, or a year and a half—this was the extent of that.
And I started working in the Bureau of Indian Affairs in 1938 and have been
around the Bureau for thirty-some years now. Starting from Rosebud agency
for a short period of time, I moved to Washington—transferred to central
office in Washington, D.C. I spent about ten years in there, then went to
various places, at various levels. From there, I went back to the reservation area—Turtle Mountain—and was administrative officer for about two
years. Then to Pine Ridge. I was over at Pine Ridge for two years or so,
and then from there I moved into the area office-level down in Andarko,
Oklahoma. I was there for about three years, and moved over to Muskogee,
Oklahoma. I was in another area office and was there for about nine years.
And then, from there, up here. I've been here about seven years. That's kind
of a resume of my service in the Bureau.

I remember [when the Indian Reorganization Act was applied out at
Rosebud] I never had too much contact before with the agency. We always
lived way out in the country, and our contacts with the Bureau at that time

133

were what you would call farm agents, or boss farmer. These were aban-
doned districts, in the outlying areas of the reservations. They would come
around and keep us informed and deal with leases and things of this sort.

We lived in a community where there was quite a number of Indian
families, many of whom were my relatives. They were quite politically-
minded—tribally, politically-minded. I remember them talking about this
New Deal that was coming out at that time. Of course, this was in administration of a Franklin D. Roosevelt, and his new Commissioner, John Collier,
who immediately proposed to Congress a new era for the American Indian
people. He proposed to Congress this legislation.

This was a new deal for the Indians. Nobody really understood it.
They knew that they were going to have to vote on whether they wanted
it or not. Of course, it was very difficult many times to get things accurately
to them. It was a matter of communication—very difficult because they
would interpret in many ways the minor things. They had all kinds of
stories going about the new program. Many were against, and many were
for it. From what they understood of it, it was very difficult because it was
such a radical change from their way of life. Really, their customs and
practices up to that point—most all of their governing procedures in the
tribe—were handled through tribal leaders, designated by the chiefs, the
leaders from one generation to another. They looked to the tribal chiefs, or
leaders, to guide them in their procedures. They had no formal government
of any kind, though they were fairly well organized.

Anyway, this was quite a radical change to bolt on. I think many of
them looked at this as another way for Government to take over more of
their controls. But finally, the Bureau got going on this, and organized themselves fairly well, and established some positions as to the responsibilities of
employees. They would go around to explain the Reorganization Act to the
people on all the reservations as best they could. I remember the one on
Rosebud—the reorganization man, they called him—was Mr. Ben Reifel. He
was a man who had been in Washington working for the Bureau and was
very capable. He was selected as one of these men to go out in the Rosebud area and explain this—sell it in other words. So he did. He spent quite
a lot of time there. Then, finally, they were given deadlines or dates to vote.
I don't remember all the details on that, but I think they had a rather close
vote, as I recall, on adopting the Reorganization Act on the Rosebud Reservation.

Of course, the point of interest was it had a lot of advantages, in that
many of the people would have loan funds available—huge amounts. Farm
programs were developed through this; cattle-ranging programs were initiated. Educational loans were beginning to be made available for the
Indian youngsters who had never had any opportunity before to attend
higher institutions. There was a new feeling there in education. And, of
course, mainly the tribal governing body got busy there and established the

governing body, voted on their representatives and their council members. It was, I think, difficult for the people to recognize what they were doing for probably several years, until they got into the change.

HERBERT HOOVER   Ben Reifel was a fairly effective salesman, then?

A   My own personal opinion is, probably if it wasn't for him—if he hadn't represented the Bureau—it would have been very unlikely that this would have been effective. Because he could speak the language, and he knew the people and had many relatives and friends on the reservation. It made it easier for him to get the program across, and I think that this had a lot to do with it.

I don't believe that this particular reservation [Winnebago] did too much in utilizing their resources. They had some very valuable land here, on this reservation, farm land in an intensive farm area. They have very good land. Maybe those days, that is forty years ago, farming wasn't as productive and great as it is today. And, of course, forty years ago they were just beginning a complete change as happened on the Rosebud Reservation. It took several years for them to realize that they were in a new type of situation.

Still, on this reservation, like there, maybe many people felt like there has not been much progress. But there really has, when you look and compare thirty years ago—with the materialistic things. In many other ways they haven't progressed—in the human resource side. Much of that, I think, is natural. They have resisted. They wanted to retain their status as tribal people—Winnebagos—on this reservation. I think this is probably true across the nation, as far as American Indians are concerned. Many people make comparisons with the dominant society, or the non-Indian, and say, "See, there is no progress here. They are worse off than they were fifty years ago." Well, it depends upon what you are trying to compare with. The way I see it, you are trying to compare it with the dominant society, and this has been the policy of the Bureau of Indian Affairs—to make them more like the non-Indian. This has been the source of great resistance with most tribes in the plains area. They have resisted the attempt in many cases. Take the next reservation south, the Omahas. They have resisted, and it's very evident in their tribe today. Compare them with the Winnebago, and probably—on the surface—it appears that they are not as far advanced in being like the dominant society. It is going on today. They are attempting to resist, especially the older generation. The younger people in elementary and secondary schools, that are living here on the reservation, are kind of being caught up in the whiplash of this. I think they are in the era of transition, caught in between, because their middle-aged parents many times are still resistant against the efforts of teaching from the dominant society. Yet, they still believe in education, and this kind of confuses things.

Q   How do people here earn their livings?

A   Like most all reservations, they are all pretty much falling in the category of being poverty-stricken people. Their income is primarily from lease-rentals here on the reservation land; this applies to people who are in the elderly group, or in the middle-aged group, and have income from land. The other people have no land, unless they inherited it. Some have incomes from spot jobs or part-time work—generally unskilled, agricultural work. Even that is fading out, now. In the five to seven years that I have been here, there has been a tremendous reduction, because of the great increase in single ownership of farms. And the going to mechanization of farms has greatly reduced this hand labor that they were accustomed to doing. Some work in industry at Sioux City, or in the nearby areas.

I think the significant thing about this, the entire Winnebago population, is that we have about two thousand members on the vast Winnebago rolls. There are approximately seven hundred people living on the reservation here in Nebraska. So you can see, almost two-thirds of these people —or sixty percent of these people—are gone. They have, to a great extent on their own initiative, left here for better opportunities. They are living in all parts of the country. So what we are dealing with here locally are these approximately seven hundred people. You analyze these and you find that a great percentage—over fifty percent of these—are elderly people. And these people, of course, are living on some type of welfare—old age, social security, veterans benefits, plus some other kinds of income—small income. These people are living on this type of income because of their age and their being unskilled, besides uneducated. A great percentage of these are going to be in this category of low income regardless—from now on—until they pass on. Then you have another maybe twenty-five percent that are children of school age—children that are living with parents, or grandparents, or relatives. We have another maybe ten percent more of a people who are disabled and unable to work. Or, if they are able to work, they are unskilled and have no ability to get a job. Then some are handicapped in other ways.

A final thing about the work force here. We are out making the effort, like we are on most reservations, to get industry located on or near the reservation employment. This low income is not necessarily due to the high rate of unemployment. It is due to these other factors. But we do have an unemployed force here—one hundred people as workers for an industry.

Of course, many of the Winnebagos living in the urban centers are probably far worse off than various people here. We may not have the best housing. We have a housing situation that is very critical here, too. Income may not be as great, but they do have a lot of freedom here as far as open spaces, clean air, and sanitary facilities in these homes. They do have things of this type. Many of the people living in the urban centers are finding real difficulty because they are handicapped leaving here with very limited education. They obtained some kind of a skill when they went away on training, but maybe that skill has depleted itself. I know many a person on the

West Coast where the technology changes the skill—it becomes obsolete. They are immediately out of a job and living in pretty bad circumstances. Many of these people would come back to the reservation if there was any kind of hope or possibility of them being able to find permanent employment. Now if the tribe were fortunate enough to establish and develop resources and with our [the Government's] assistance were able to locate some kind of a permanent industry here that would employ men and women, it would be a good possibility that it would bring quite a few back. I think the tribe is looking in this direction. They are presently developing an industrial park here, on tribal land, south of the village in Winnebago. This will be an excellent spot for industry and there have been several contacts already for locating industries. Locating industries on the reservation is not the answer to all the problems. It is one of the things that helps, though.

Of course, we have people coming back here periodically to retire —independent people coming back home after many years of being away to live among and with their relatives and just be here. This kind of offsets itself with the leaving and the coming up to this point, because this figure I quoted (approximately seven hundred people) has been rather constant for several years—maybe ten years or so. There hasn't been any great loss in the past several years.

If they would develop some opportunities here—get industry and some tribal enterprises, or something, it could provide some opportunities for some of their skilled and uneducated people to come back. This is something that the tribal council is dreaming now. They would like to have their people back here.

Someone needs to do a considerable amount of work in the social area. Throughout our office, we have two social workers on our staff that are professional social workers. I would like to see half a dozen more trained social workers around the reservation and start on a concentrated effort to take a certain number of families and start working with these people. I am speaking, for example, in the area of what used to be known as Indian custom marriages, or common-law marriages. There is not much of this going on at this time. But we are getting the results of some that happened twenty years ago. Indian youngsters are being denied many benefits because of inability to determine who their parents are. Along with this is a problem of alcoholism. This has created a real severe situation on both reservations —Omaha and Winnebago. This, of course, is not due to the fact that these are Indian people. This is a poverty problem, the same thing in urban centers today, and in the ghettos, and everywhere else. But what we are talking about here now—we certainly need to start developing some programs to overcome such needs on the reservations . . . .

Another area of big concern is education. In Nebraska we have no Bureau schools. They are all public schools. All the youngsters that attend school in Nebraska, on each reservation, attend public schools. We have contracts with the state of Nebraska whereby we pay for tuition, transportation, lunches, and special services for the Indian people. There are four schools where we provide contract services—Winnebago, Macy, Walt Hill, and Niobrara. For the Winnebago school, I'd say nearly eighty percent of the total funds provided come from federal funds . . . . In checking into the school system, it was an accredited school system all right, but there was great lack of academic training for Indian youngsters. They just were not getting it. They weren't making any efforts to try and cope with acute problems involved in the education of Indian youngsters—they didn't understand. Academically, he was just pushed along, or he was just a dropout . . . .

In general, medical services here in Winnebago have been very good. The hospital is generally well staffed. Of course, your medical officers generally are young, recent graduates from medical school with very little experience. However, they are able to do general practice and gain experience at the same time. I don't necessarily believe in this type of medical treatment for American Indians. I think they are entitled to better services than this. I mean, they should be given the best type of services possible, in the same way as with education. They are entitled to the best the Government is paying for. This they pay for—the best, but they don't get it in many instances. In my opinion, our education here in this area is very poor for the money that they pay them. I think this is true in the medical area. I think they pay for the best, but they are not getting the best. They get the best they can get, this is what it amounts to. Public health service can't get doctors like a lot of communities who pay a lot of money . . . .

Q   What did you think of the Government's relocation program of the 1950s?

A   In the early fifties there was a lot of pressure placed on the people. It was always considered a voluntary program, but there was a lot of promotion of the program in the early stages. I know from my own experience that this program . . . known as the relocation program was started in the early fifties when I was at Pine Ridge. We were one of the first to have a relocation officer, and in order to get the thing going (it was kind of a crash program) we just went out and rounded them up in trucks. "You want to go to California, or somewhere and get a job?" "Sure!" Everybody was jumping on the bandwagon. They wanted the trip, or something, so a lot of it was confusion.

This is true with a lot of new programs. To get a crash thing going, Congress gives you money. They want results, you know, right away. By the time you go back next year for your new funding, you better have some results to show. Or they say, "We gave you money for this, and how come all of this didn't happen?" You know, to get a new program going you have to hire specialized people. There are a thousand different things you have to do. The first year or two are more or less chaos, to get a program of that size off the ground.

A lot of the people were pushed into this program to begin with. This is the reason the return rate was so high, to begin with—probably fifty percent or more. It still today runs one-third, even if it is a voluntary program. I think the greatest determinant is the fact that the individual is just not able to adjust himself to the community, the urban center. The reason they return is because they just can't make it from a standpoint of being able to accustom themselves to urban living. In addition, generally it is because their skill is just not great enough to provide an average standard of living. They would have to slip down into a lower-class living. They have a program where they won't let them get down into the ghetto area to live. But after they once get on their own, they can't control them. And then they go back down there, or they give up and go back to the reservation. To me, I would rather live on the reservation than some of those ghetto areas that they are forced into. I certainly don't condemn anyone for coming back to the reservation. I know quite a bit about city areas. I think that many of these people who are being sent out are just not going to make it because first of all, their educational level is low. In many instances, even with the best training you can get based on educational level, they will have a real tough time in this day and age making it in many urban centers with the competition. I have talked to and seen many from each of the reservations that are living in urban centers, like on the coast—Los Angeles, San Francisco, and those areas. I know of one successful young couple, probably in their forties, who are Omahas. They have been out in Los Angeles for twelve or thirteen years now. They were sent out on the relocation program. He received training out there as a welder; he is a master welder now, and he makes real good money where he works. He has worked for several companies, first one, then another. He is doing all right, because he was one that was able to come out as a master welder. Not too many make that. I know several others that are just barely making it—moving from one payday to another, so to speak. They have thousands of problems, problems involved in education with children, community problems moving in in certain areas, restricted areas, and all. This is another confusing thing to many Indian people, their being unable to live in certain areas that they would like to live in and could afford to live in. In many places they are unable to do this. On the reservation, they don't get into this. They can live where they want to.

Amos Owen

Mdewakanton Sioux

Prairie Island Indian Community, Minnesota
Interviewed by Herbert T. Hoover
June 24, 1970

Mr. Owen was tribal chairman for Prairie Island Indian Community
and fifty-three years old at the time of this interview.

HERBERT HOOVER How have the Indians of Prairie Island fared
economically in your lifetime?

AMOS OWEN I was born and raised on the Sisseton Reservation in
South Dakota. My father was from there, and my mother was from this
territory here. I lived out there until after my father died, and then I
moved back out here with my mother. And I've been here ever since . . .
1933.

It was 1934 when the Wheeler-Howard Act came into effect—otherwise known as the Indian Reorganization Act. Most of the small reservations in Minnesota came under this bill, accepted and adopted the
Wheeler-Howard Act. So, of course, Prairie Island was one of the first to
go under it. We thought it was a good way for the American Indians to be
self-supporting, and to be able to get a little more land and be able to
farm the land that they have. The Wheeler-Howard Act bought up
I think, 300 or 380 acres of land out here. My brother and I, we were some
of the ones that went into farming in 1938. We farmed until all of us left
for World War II.

But the act didn't pan out as we thought it was going to. Of course,
I was pretty young at the time. But I remember when we first organized,
the Wheeler-Howard Act was . . . I guess originally really good. If the
Indians made a little money they could buy up more land. That was the
way the act was written up, before it went through Congress. It was

140

revised a bit, so that buying that land was struck out of the papers ... it it wasn't in the charter and the constitution and bylaws when the thing came into effect.

There were farming loans; we had farming loans. That was the only benefit we got out of the Wheeler-Howard Act. We bought machinery and livestock and things that are beneficial to the community. In fact, they were all personal loans to families. So the act helped some of the families out here to get started in farming. And they farmed until one of them died, and the others got pretty old and then would just quit.

They had this Civilian Conservation Corps that the Department of the Interior put out. That was for everybody—they could work on the reservation. They had jobs, such as road repairs and stuff like that. It gave everybody employment. It kept the married families working. The money wasn't much. But a dollar went a little farther way back then.

After World War II, there was a long stretch in there—twenty years —before they [the Government] ever did anything down here again. That's when we got the new housing and things. But they were all different—from different branches of Government. I can't say the Bureau of Indian Affairs neglects us; it isn't bad. But, of course, a little reservation like this—they don't hear from us so they think we are all right. I think somebody should write a letter every week, so they know what our needs are.

Northern States Power Company has been a big factor as far as jobs go [construction work, in the erection of the nuclear generating plant on the edge of the community]. I think most of the able-bodied men of the community are working down there now. I don't know just how many, but we have had just about every man available go down there and they have put them all on. So I think it is really a big help to the community. It really gave us a big hand by giving everybody a job. I don't think there have been many working at [nearby] Red Wing [where there exist at least six vigorous industrial plants]; I think there are only one or two that work in Red Wing now.

Bill O'Connor

Yankton Sioux

Yankton Reservation, South Dakota
Interviewed by Joseph H. Cash
Summer 1968

———

Mr. O'Connor was in his seventies at the time of this interview.

———

JOSEPH H. CASH Do you remember anything about them trying to put in the Indian Reorganization Act back in the thirties?

BILL O'CONNOR The Reorganization Act, as I know it, opened up different avenues of life to develop themselves socially, economically, and other aspects which are important to any civilized country. The Indians were so remote at the time, and during that period, especially the thirties, the times were very deplorable, and there were hopes that they could live better, change the living conditions; and that was the hope of me, as I saw it, because the times were rough. The period when the grasshoppers invaded the country here, they devoured all vegetation, and then the decline of the Indian health was so noticeable at that time.

Q How was it noticeable?

A Well, the noticeable malnutrition, because of these times, it brought on conditions where food was so scarce. That's how this Indian hospital here at Wagner was built, because of the health conditions here, they warranted such an action.

The Reorganization Act, the Yankton people accepted the act itself; however, to go another step forward to complete it, they have failed to adopt a suitable constitution. I think two constitutions were turned down, because there was a lot of rivalry. And some of the Indian politicians said that this kind of an action would be a detriment to the Indian people. So they balked, and the result is that the Indians of the Yankton Reservation have never adopted a constitution under the act. They have a constitution

142

now; they're functioning with it, but they stated when the constitution was drawn up that this is not a constitution under the Reorganizaion Act: It was very brief and stated so.

The Reorganization Act has been accepted. Personally, as a layman, I'm saying that the Indians of the Yankton Sioux tribe are under the act, because they have accepted the act; but it has always been said that they are an unorganized tribe. I don't go along with that, because they have accepted the act, even though they have a constitution now stating it's not under the Reorganization Act. But the main thing is they are under the act itself, the big law they're right under. Of course, the law itself as I understand it as a layman, there are provisions in there which would have been fully enjoyed if the Indians would have completed in the entirety of it, which they haven't, and for that reason I think many of the benefits have never fully been enjoyed.

They should have drawn up a constitution whereby they could declare it fully—"This is a constitution under the Reorganization Act of 1934." They should have been very specific there in saying and declaring this, which they never did. I've always been under the assumption that this statute would be of great value to my Yankton Sioux people, and I have always been more or less regretful that they have never been able to understand it fully so that they could cherish such a move, where they could have been able to enjoy more. That I do regret.

Q Do you remember how they were trying to get that act put through? Did they have meetings back in 1934 or whenever it was?

A I like that question. There's something that I want to say now, as this is going to be recorded, and as I know, perhaps this will never come this way again. This Reorganization Act was explained to the Indian people, and since the conditions heretofore mentioned by me, like the great grasshopper plague of that period, and drought conditions, those conditions would naturally make people desperate, and anything that promises hope will be fully accepted. Well, such was the case.

When it was brought to the Indian people and explained, many of the horses had died, only here and there were there horses left. There was hardly any vegetation, any grass, so naturally, the horses starved to death. And one man, by the name of Ahmet, he was quite a forceful speaker, and he said, "There will be horses bought and brought in here for you Indian people, and there will be milk cows brought in here for you Indian people. There will be chickens in every backyard." Now, such talk is very inducing, and naturally when it came up to be decided by vote, why it was, you might say, over half for it, and it was accepted. And everything seemed to be all right until it came to drafting the constitution. There was a lot of rivalry there, in writing and drafting this constitution, and in the meantime, they brought in outsiders to promote this.

Outsiders, that is to say, from Rosebud; and that caused hostility. See, the Indians here can become hostile. Some of them thought, "Well, we are capable in doing this, because it concerns us. Why should we have some people dictate to us, the conditions we like to live under?" So they got hostile. Now these people—I'd like to mention them. One is dead now—Guy Lambert was one, he was the chief of police from Rosebud. And Ben Reifel, the congressman now; he was the BIA official at that time. I don't know in what capacity he worked, what title he was under. But anyway, they were outside of this reservation, and I think at this time that in reviewing the whole thing, such action hurt the Indian people to decide on this drafting of the constitution. And when it was, it was turned down because of that reason. They resented the outside pressure, and inasmuch as it was defeated, it wasn't defeated by very much. I think something like twenty-odd votes. So since that time—it has been over thirty years now—and we have been going along, inasmuch as we are under the Reorganization Act, we still live this way.

Q Do you remember who the people were who opposed the act, or the ones that supported it? There must have been some leaders around.

A Yes. The opposing forces, Henry Fredrick was one of the opposers, and my friend over here, Clarence Foreman is one, to name just a few that were very effective in the opposing forces. Of course, there were others, too, but these were the most destructive ones, I would say. And Clement Smith. And I think these three I mentioned were the most effective ones.

And those who tried to promote the Reorganization Act, perhaps I will say I was one of them, because from this action I was called a dictator and a big crook and other things which doesn't justify because there's nothing I derived from it. I just got a lot of abuse out of something that I'd hoped for for our Indian people. So really, I'm free to say, my conscience is clear, that there's nothing that I derived from the Reorganization Act, only a couple of ponies that I think I got out of the deal. And, of course, I had to pay for them, too. They were purchased with a loan.

Q Who called you these things?

A Well, at different meetings when I spoke there in favor of the Reorganization Act, why others would take the floor and they'd say, "Bill O'Connor is trying to say this way of life is good, because he's trying to promote his own interests, and that's all." Really, it doesn't justify that. I'm in about the same circumstances I am right now as I was at that time when I spoke.

Q You had a series of meetings in which you kind of debated this?

A Oh, yes. Prior to bringing in the Reorganization Act, explaining the benefits that can be derived, and after the act was accepted, and then to draft the constitution which was turned down, and it took a series of meetings for that, and another draft was made, and that took several meetings, and that was turned down.

Q Then you had two attempts to get organized?

A   Yes, two attempts that I know that were worthwhile were turned down, and from that time on, why it kind of died out. That was a good deal—like the Battle of Wounded Knee, it kind of killed the whole thing.

These meetings were held in all parts of the reservation. Of course, this area here where I'm speaking from is the White Swan area, this is the White Swan district. And in this area, we had a meeting hall, and there was where a lot of these preliminary meetings were held to condition for the resolution that was coming up which took the action of the tribal council. After a proper representative, representation from each district, and also those interested enough would go down there and act upon these resolutions at the general council.

Q   Would all the Indians come from all over the reservation?

A   Well, I can't say all of them, because there are always factors in any case, and that's this transportation problem. Some of them didn't have transportation and at that time a lot of them were being transported down here. Of course, at that time I think there were funds available, I don't know just exactly from what source, but they furnished cars and gasoline, and they were transported down there so that votes could be taken.

Usually some BIA official would call the meeting to order and he would ask them to nominate somebody that would chair the meeting, and a secretary and so forth, which would be temporary.

Q   Did you have to use interpreters back then?

A   Yes, in those days, interpreters were necessary.

Q   Then they held a series of meetings like this all over the reservation, at Greenwood and other places?

A   Yes, to begin with there were three districts—the White Swan district, the Greenwood district, and the Shelby Creek district. It was necessary that these local districts would have an audience of some kind where the speakers could speak to them to explain as they know it. Each district had a powerful opposing man speaker and there's always been a promoter for the Reorganization Act, too, in each district. So it's pretty hard to make a division there.

Q   Was there a difference between older people and younger people regarding this act?

A   Now, of course, the older ones, naturally they were frightened by such talk, saying that if you accept the Reorganization Act your real estate holdings will be in jeopardy. The younger ones are more for such an opportunity. They are the ones who will cause your downfall. And naturally the younger ones classified themselves as the new dealers and the older ones were classified as the old dealers. The older ones are the ones who receive allotments, whereas the younger ones were never allotted. Of course, the younger ones that have any land obtained it through inheritance, but these older ones, they were the allottees, and such talk that their holdings would be in jeopardy, this kind of action would be a detriment to them. They kind of balked on it. The ones who said that their real estate holdings would be in jeopardy were the ones who seemed to be the ones who read the act and who were told by other sources that the Reorganization Act was no good. "This is the action of the white man, that he's going to close on you. This is a law, a legal way to bleed you to death and bring you to an end."

I can truthfully say that it has done good. It could have done more if it was fully exercised, and I think it's never been exercised to the fullest. It gave him self-government, it gave back the incentive the Indian had lost, and he could have developed that more. Of course, many realize that now and in this stage now, the reservation is being more or less revised. I don't know whether it is an action of reprisal that the Yankton Sioux Reservation —that is the agency—was abolished, maybe as a reprisal for not accepting the Reorganization Act. It was said the abolishment of the Yankton agency was an economy move. And I don't hardly agree to that, because at the time when they had abolished the agency, they had seven employees. Now they have eleven on the staff at the sub-agency here at Wagner. Of course, recently the agency is back to full status; it has been restored. Now they have a tribal government here, but with a constitution that is weak, so to speak, because it doesn't carry the statutory powers under the Reorganization Act. They should declare it fully that this is under the Reorganization Act.

John Stricker

Yankton Sioux

Yankton Reservation, South Dakota
Interviewed by Joseph H. Cash
Summer 1968

Mr. Stricker was thirty-four years old when interviewed. Since
that time he has started a national Indian organization.

JOSEPH H. CASH   Mr. Stricker, I understand that you're quite active
in tribal politics. Is that correct?

JOHN STRICKER   Yes, I have been ever since I came back to the
reservation from the service when I was in the Army. Oh, it's been eleven
years ago. And there's a lot of straightening up that there has to be done—
economically, politically and that; and our laws and that which pertain to
our way of living, and laws that are on Indian law books that the white
man doesn't know about. We're not really living by them. But in that way,
we're in between two worlds—a white world and an Indian world—and you
just can't seem to make things work. And lawyers try to help us, but it
takes them two or three years to really study what the problem is and
then to find out what's going on. Like if I have a problem on the Indian
reservation, I go to the white lawyer and he can't take the case right away,
because he's got to look back into the federal statute books on Indian law
and that, which means you're held up again, economically-wise, whether
it's an economic decision to be made or whether just a plain decision on
law and order.

It's a problem that all the young Indians have to face, but how to
settle it—that's another question.

Q   What are these problems do you think?

A   Well, one of them is that our tribes always have been really independent. The white man understands his laws as being regulated by the
United States Constitution and through the courts and that. Well, we

147

have always believed that in our Indian way, and thereby we never buckled under to any 1934 act or any program, because we have always felt that the individual's rights should be protected even if it meant starvation or lack of programs, which we do have. I mean, everything we've got is phased out now on the economic level of the Government programs.

You have to go back and study, like the guy who wrote it—Collier—and other fellows. Now there again, to me, it would be just one big communal system like China and that. Like you say, I'm more educated than my fathers were, and I've done a lot more traveling, and I've talked to a lot more people, and I've always been good in history and that, regardless, whether it's white man's history of the Indian history and that. Now if you go back to our 1934 act, I'm not saying that nothing good can become of it—but the thing there is that we had farming possibilities before the 1934 act came in. But there again it's economical, like you had your drought coming in the same time, in the thirties, and you had the 1934 act on top of it, which you had to comply with regulations and laws of the Bureau, which means that everything had to be . . . they regulated everything, see. Right now it ain't so bad, like you talk to our fathers. When they wanted to go over here to visit their relations over at Fort Thompson, you had to have a pass to go there. They just couldn't leave the reservation, see; things like that.

Like right now, sure, they have good points on the Rosebud and Oglala reservations, but if they want to take your land and put it in the land program, there is nothing to do about it, see. As an individual you have to go according to the wishes of your tribal laws and your constitution. So our constitutions are outdated, too, as Indians, as far as giving us our rights. We say the white man is violating our rights, but we as Indians, ourselves, we have ambitious Indians that would become dictators on the reservation and deny us our own rights. Like right now, this 1934 act—you could farm when they told you to farm. You had to buy your seed when they told you to buy, which means you were always a week or a month behind planting season. You can't do business that way. And your horses had to be bought from the Bureau, everything had to be bought from them, and we had one guy here, it was the last superintendent we had. He was kicked completely out of the Bureau because he would go down in Iowa and places and buy these old nags that weren't worth anything and come back and sell them to an Indian at such a price, where he was making money on them. If I put you in business, if you wanted to go into business with me backing you, you had to do everything my way, and if I didn't know anything about your business and how you'd run it and I just told you how to run it, you would soon go bankrupt, Boy, and that was the way it was with the Indian. He couldn't manage his own affairs under the 1934 act. It was done on the communal system.

Everybody was supposed to do their work, and then at the end of the season, everybody gets paid, see. It won't work for us. It'll work for maybe Mennonites, and on people on that social level, you know. They believe in that type of living. I say it's up to the white man; he's going to solve it—the voters of the state and that. We're going to have to sell the story to them. It's not whether they know the laws or not. It's whether they can have them interpreted for the betterment of the Indian economically and politically. Because, you have no appeal courts, because the Indian is too poor to go to have his decision appealed. And he's found guilty without even going to court. And these things here were all brought along by the 1934 act, from which we never not anything, because our fathers said they didn't want the 1934 act. And to me, there was some good in it, even if we had to buckle under certain conditions—but now there isn't. There is no possibility under it, because all your programs are fizzled out, bankrupt under the 1934 act. So right now there wouldn't be anything that we would gain by it as young Indians under it.

You take some Bureau officials, they say that we don't have to pay gratuity back. Gratuity means like if you were an Indian and I gave you a horse, and I gave you flour, and I gave you salted pork to live on, and not much more, and I say it's a gift for you because you signed a treaty, but then I turned around and said you had to pay me back if you ever got on your feet. Now that's the same thing they're telling the Indian. They're saying that we don't have to pay them back, see. But down and around they are.

All the way back to your dried apples back at that time, when I was a little kid I passed them out for the older people, and everything came in wooden barrels then. All that's considered gratuity, and everything they did for the Indians is gratuity. That's what they're saying, and under the 1934 act it states right in there that they can do it.

We were one of the last three tribes that could negotiate our own contracts, like a businessman of the white world. But we have lost that even, because the Indians—through the lack of education—they gave that up to the lawyer, because the lawyer was smart. When we brought up the laws in the books, the treaty laws and that, the lawyer said, "Oh, we don't go by that." But after the meeting was over, we backed him down, because it's the law in the book. It's not whether I put it there, or whether I live by it. The law states it's a law, and then if I'm an Indian, then I live by it. And I think he should live by it, if it is Indian law.

Q   Do you think that the Bureau discriminates against you, because you refuse to go under the act?

A   Well, I know they do. Like I say, there are Indians that discriminate against Indians themselves on the color of their skins, like you say the Negro have the same problems—the dark skin with the lighter skin. I went up to Pierre here, to see about our school down here that closed. Under the treaty, it states that we have a right to say whether our schools close or not. We have a right to say whether the schools stay open and that. We have a right to say how we want our education, and that's one of the main stipulations of the treaty—education. But they didn't give us any voting right on it or anything. They just came in and said they were going to close it.

Q   Is this a Bureau school at Greenwood?

A   It used to be. It was financed by the Federal Government. So I went up there and this guy didn't know I was on the tribal council—he was sitting out there. He said he didn't like to work with the Winnebagos; he didn't know I'm not a Winnebago. He said, "Well, because they're mixed, they're intermixed with Negro now." And to me it doesn't make any difference whether you're intermixed with Negro, white, or anything. If you're on the reservation, the law states that if you're living with an Indian mother or Indian father, you are entitled to these privileges. But these guys here, they discriminate against various tribes, and that's what is happening to us, because we haven't the means to hire a good lawyer to present our case. We have no means to really fight anybody in the courts, and that's the only way you can do business in our country, I mean justly, without going to arms and that, you know, like the Negro's doing. The Indians don't believe in that. We believe that it should be done through process of law, but we're so poor that we can't go through the process of law, because we have no means to do it. And it takes money.

Harold Schunk

Yankton Sioux

Rosebud Reservation, South Dakota
Interviewed by Joseph H. Cash
Summer 1967

Mr. Schunk has been a Bureau of Indian Affairs executive for many years and was superintendent of several reservations, including Cheyenne River, Turtle Mountain, and Rosebud. Now retired, he lectures extensively and serves on boards and committees on the local, state, and national level. He was sixty-one years old at the time of this interview.

HAROLD SCHUNK   You have asked me the question how the Indians fared during the Depression. This is my own personal opinion; I think when times are tough, possibly the Indian fares better than he does when times are good. The Depression came along, and I believe, for the first time in Indian history, everybody got to work. Back in the old CCC [Civilian Conservation Corps] days, I started at Rosebud in 1933, on June the sixth. I had just been out of college two years. I was placed in charge of two CCC camps, one a few miles up from old Highway 18, the other located at where the Spring Creek Day School is now. This gave the Indian the opportunity to go to work. I actually knew a great many fellows who had never had a steady job. This gave them an opportunity to have a steady job. I recall talking to many individuals who had only worked very spasmodically, and most of them at that time had worked on ranches and farms. This gave them an opportunity to work. It also gave them an opportunity to get in on some of the new developments at that time, like housing, which was carried on throughout the CCC program. Irrigation was set up where they had quite a sizeable acreage of irrigated land along the Big White River. They also had a few cattle and did some milking. They had a few hogs. They had chickens. The extension service at that time was very active.

Also, at Grass Mountain—which is along the Little White River south and west of the agency—they had another irrigated setup. They also had stock programs. They had cattle programs throughout the reservation. Each individual would get so many repayment cattle. For example, we say a man would get thirty repayment cattle, they would give him in the neighborhood of six to eight years to pay back the thirty head. He had no interest to pay, but just in kind, in other words. This seemed to work out fairly well at the time. We must remember back in those days a man's wants are a lot simpler than they are today. Today a man has to have three hundred head of cattle to make a decent living, where at that time he could do it with seventy-five or a hundred; he could get along quite well. In fact, when I left here in December the first of 1934, I would say at least eighty percent of these people were still using the team and wagon. Today, you rarely ever see a team and wagon. You'd want to stop and take a picture of it if you had a camera. There are so many things to tell about those times.

I recall some of the boys that I had in camp. Quite a number of them I had went on and became very successful individuals. They took advantage of the opportunities that were there at that time—the training and the education—they could go on and make something of themselves.

JOSEPH H. CASH   Did you find that these Indian boys would work on a steady, responsible basis?

A   We found a great many of them. I think they would compare to the average American, in responsibility. When they once got started, we did a great deal of work around here. We have some beautiful dams that were built back at that time that are still here. Naturally, we did a lot of work that we shouldn't have done, to make work for example. One of the sad things about our program was the fact that they cut literally hundreds and hundreds of trees out of our reserve that should have never been cut.

In those days, as you know, if you can remember, the country was pretty damn dry. One of the things I always recall was a real good old friend of mine at the Cheyenne River agency. He was a real old-timer. He was eighty-five or -six when he died in 1938. He said to me, "Mr. Schunk," he said, "we're all on the same level now. The white man is in the same shape we are," which was literally true. The drought had just wiped everything out. And the old man was a real fine gentleman. We were all on the same plane at that time. It was low years, and all kinds of professional men were working on WPA [Works Progress Administration]. It was an unfortunate thing, I felt, because the more ability you had and the more education, it meant very little right at that particular time because times were tough—with the drought and everything, the Depression. But I felt that the thing that the Indian did was very good.

Clarence Foreman

Yankton Sioux

Yankton Reservation, South Dakota
Interviewed by Joseph H. Cash
Summer 1968

Mr. Foreman has long been an expert on the Yankton claims
against the United States. He was seventy-six at the time of this
interview.

CLARENCE FOREMAN   The reservation as a whole was terminated by
the treaty of 1892, whereby the Yankton Indians disposed of all their sur-
plus unallotted lands, and by that treaty the only lands that were reserved
were those lands that were reserved for agency schools and other purposes,
to be used by the Government for the administrative purposes of the
Yankton Sioux Indians. But since then, of course, the allotments that were
made to the Indians under the 1887 allotment act have also diminished. A
lot of those allotments have been sold, in accordance with the treaty agreement, and naturally the Indian landholdings became less and less. I believe
we have about as small an amount of land as any tribe in South Dakota,
anyway. I'm not familiar with other tribes.

JOSEPH H. CASH   Mr. Foreman, would you like to discuss the Indian
Reorganization Act, the so-called Wheeler-Howard Act on the Yankton
Reservation?

A   I've had so many controversial arguments over that. I've been
opposed to the act ever since its enactment.

Q   Why were you against it?

A   Well, in the beginning, we might go back to the old system of the
Bureau of Indian Affairs, whereby the Indians were doing perhaps the best
that they could do with what they had to do it with. It seemed to me, and
still seems to me, that going back to the older times when the Indians
were given their allotments and supervised by the Bureau of Indian Affairs,

that at that time, those people were making some progress. We used to have to encourage the economic side of it, the programs, and they were usually headed by the Indian people themselves. They used to have Indian fairs that would demonstrate what the Indian was doing to help himself in the way of agriculture and domestic affairs, and they were doing really well. Some of our Indian people had nice homes, beautiful homes. Some of the nicest homes in Charles Mix County at one time were Indian homes, such as the St. Pierre home and the John Omaha home. There's just a few of those, but there were some very nice homes, well kept, and the Indians were doing well.

They were industrious—these fairs that we held at that time seemed to be something to lead them, to help them do better and exhibit their crops and livestock, and they were doing really well. As far as you could judge it, what they exhibited for their work and for a better way of living was equal to that of the white man, comparatively. But it appeared to me, and this is my basic reason for opposing the Wheeler-Howard Act, that bringing about this Wheeler-Howard Act put an end to the effort that was being made by the Indian people to come up to the standards equal to that of the white man. I may have been mistaken, but I don't think I am, and I'll still stay by my decision and conviction—that it appeared to me that the Indian was making such progress that it appeared to the BIA and those that are affiliated with it that if they allowed the program that the Indians were under at that time to continue, that those fellows would soon lose their jobs, that the Indian would gradually—and most probably in a very few years—accomplish what they had set out for—their goal—that they would become self-supporting.

There was hardly a family of Indians on the reservation that I knew at that time that weren't making progress by their own effort. Farming and raising livestock and doing everything that our present farmers are doing. And since the enactment of the Wheeler-Howard Act, the Indian has been turned right around the other way. You don't find the progress any more that the Indians were making. They just dumped the plow over to one side and threw up their hands and said, "Well, we'll just wait and see what this New Deal is going to do for us." And it didn't do very much.

Q   Do you think it was Wheeler-Howard that stopped their progress or was it the Depression?

A   Well, we'll admit that we've had depressions such as the droughts and wars and so on, but nevertheless, the whole system was changed. The whole administration of Indian affairs was completely changed to the greatest extent. There were a few Indians that believed in the Wheeler-Howard Act, and they were organized under what is known as the rehabilitation program. There were only a small number of them included in that; it was optional whether they wanted to go into that organization or not. And, of course, there was a lot of money appropriated at different times for those fellows that were eligible to come under that Reorganization Act, but there was pressure. If they didn't happen to belong to the group that supported the program—of course, they didn't get in it, and they were left out and told that they could tighten their belts. There was a lot of pressure at that time.

I was just talking to a party a day or two ago about a man that was one of the first members of that organization, and he's still in there. He's been in there over thirty-four years, and he's no further ahead now than he was when he started. But this individual has had the benefit of everything that the Bureau could offer him and everything that the organization could offer him, and yet he's no further today than he was when he started. But because he's a strong supporter of the BIA, he's the chief of the tribe as far as that's concerned. He's the chairman of the tribe. And as far as the Wheeler-Howard Act or the new deal organization is concerned, if it had such great potentialities as to give a fellow a rehabilitation setup, it wouldn't take thirty-two years to accomplish anything, certainly.

But it's been run that way. And there are other features of the Wheeler-Howard Act—or the new deal we used to call it—that are equally shaded. Now under the old regime, we seemed to get along a lot better. As I mentioned before, there was something there—we had competition, yes, but our competition was white competition. We wanted to become self-supporting and do just as nearly as possible as the white man was doing, in order to be good citizens, self-supporting. But under the Wheeler-Howard Act, the only fellow that ever got anywhere, and he hasn't gotten anywhere yet, is the fellow that supported the BIA.

So it appears to me that if the Indian people could have continued under their old program, that they eventually would have accomplished a lot for themselves and gradually the Bureau of Indian Affairs would've run out of a job. Now you go back to 1932, when they placed the Yankton Sioux under the jurisdiction of the Rosebud agency. Well, that was under the Hoover administration. Whether or not it was a real wise step or not, I can't say, but the Indians, at that time, had a considerable amount of land, individual allotments particularly, and we only had about eight employees at the agency. We had a superintendent and an assistant, we had a boss farmer, chief clerk, lease clerk, we had a financial clerk. Well, then they placed us under the Rosebud jurisdiction; they cut that staff down to about four employees—an assistant superintendent under the jurisdiction of Rosebud and a boss farmer, and an assistant boss farmer, and a lease clerk—about four. Well, since that time, there's been a lot of land disposed of, Indian land, allotments and heirship lands, and as a result, they naturally wouldn't have as much need for more employees now than they did then. But quite contrary to that, they do have more employees now than they had then. The Indians have less. They have less land and while there are other Government agencies that are taking care of our aged—old-agers and some on social security . . . . So it appears to me that this big bug is trying to eat up the little ones in this deal. They're trying to keep something going, and I can't see to save me where these Indian people are advancing one bit.

Q   Do you think that the Indian is not making any progress?

A   No, he is absolutely not in my book. My observation is, and it always has been, that they can jerk the rug clear out from under the Bureau of Indian Affairs as far as I'm concerned, and they still would get as much care and attention, and something that would eventually lead them into a better way of life.

Q   I believe that the Yankton Sioux had their first constitution in 1932 before the Wheeler-Howard Act. Is that right?

A   Yes, the first constitution of the Yankton Sioux that was adopted —I believe it was in September in 1932. And that constitution was ratified or approved by the department, and there was a governing body elected, and they operated under that constitution.

Q   They actually had elections and a chairman, and it was a going concern?

A   That's right. And the committee that was elected under that constitution and bylaws was elected for a two-year term, and then they were to hold a new election. But that new election came up about the time the Wheeler-Howard Act had been accepted by the Yankton Indians, and for that reason the Department of Indian Affairs refused to recognize the action of the tribe in electing a new committee under the old constitution.

Q   Why did they vote to accept the IRA [Indian Reorganization Act] and then wouldn't organize?

A   Well, there was strong opposition to the Reorganization Act all the way through.

Q   Who were some of the men that opposed it?

A   Well, there were such fellows as Henry Fredrick and Clement Smith, and they were the strongest opponents; and I was one of them. There were several of those older Indian people that opposed the Wheeler-Howard Act, and they spoke violently against organizing under it. Nevertheless, when they elected a new committee under their old constitution and by-laws, I think I have the letter here from the superintendent at Rosebud. He had written in to the Commissioner, John Collier at that time, and asked what committee he would recognize here—the old committee under the old constitution and bylaws, or the new constituted committee under the Wheeler-Howard Act.

They set up what they call a rehabilitation committee, and so the Commissioner ordered him not to recognize the old committee, to recognize the new committee that was elected under the provision of the Wheeler-Howard Act, although we were not organized under it. The fact that we were not organized under it presented a problem that they at least tried to overcome by using this rehabilitation program. Of course, the rehabilitation program didn't reach everybody. It just reached its membership. Anybody that wanted to join it was treated accordingly, but it didn't reach the whole tribe. And they used that for several years, to govern the reservation and the membership of the reservation, but it finally wore out.

Finally, the rehabilitation program was discontinued, and they were put out of existence. And since that time they haven't had anything in the way of a tribal committee; they've had elections and so forth, but they claim that they are not under the Wheeler-Howard Act. In fact, the constitution and bylaws that Mr. Collier failed to recognize—in the last few years they revived that constitution.

The new deal or the Wheeler-Howard Act as we know it—I could oppose that and sit here and argue from here until Doomsday. And as my memory recalls things, I can remember a lot of things that were done, but it perhaps wasn't caused by the Wheeler-Howard Act itself, some of the things that were done. It was the political pressure and the reorganization group that was behind it that brought about a lot of hardship here on the reservation among the Indians to force them into this Reorganization Act. I have attended several hearings in Washington opposing the Wheeler-Howard Act for the Yankton Sioux. Of course, we ran into some pretty rough going there, because at that time the administration was all in favor of the Wheeler-Howard Act. But as things were organized here on the Yankton Reservation, and considering the way our Indian people were situated here, it was something that appeared to me and to others that it was something that wasn't quite acceptable to us.

The fact that we didn't have the amount of resources that were necessary to carry out some of the program, and the fact that there were other features of the Wheeler-Howard Act that had a tendency to put our Indian people back, set them back—well, I don't want to use the term like they used to use it, they used to say "Put them back under the blanket," but I don't think that it was quite that serious—but there was a tendency to stalemate the Indian right where he was at and get him to step into something that would keep him Indian forever unless he wanted to get clear off the reservation.

Q   You don't think it's desirable for him to stay Indian, as you put it?

A   Well, yes, that's my opinion. I have studied that problem of the Indian being an Indian. Certainly, we have a right; we can't help ourselves. We have a right to be an Indian as long as we are good Indians and accept the Christian civilized way of life, but we don't follow the principles that we're supposed to follow in respect to a Christian civilization, well, then we're not doing the job. But when we step back in order to keep up the powwows and a lot of these things that are more degenerating, then it does more harm than it does good. Then I would say it's about time we're jerking the rug out from some of this program.

Q   You don't like the powwows?

A   Oh, certainly not. That's just turning the Indian backwards. We have people going to these powwows, running all over the state of South Dakota to these powwows that should have stayed home and taken care of their homes, faced the winter that is coming on, and everything. They're running all over the country; these gatherings they have are not the best thing for a lot of reasons—and the drum beatings, that's all I've heard here for about three months now, drum beating and powwowing and drunken Indians. It doesn't do them any good.

Years ago, they didn't allow that. When they first started to quiet the Indian people down, they policed the reservation—they would have a policeman or two, maybe three or four—and they allowed them a dance hall. They could have an Indian dance and powwow perhaps about once a month, but that was all. The Indians were doing better then. They were doing better morally and physically, and every other way. They were getting somewhere. And this powwow, in my opinion, distracts the Indian from what he really should be looking at.

Q   Do you also oppose such things as the attempt to revive the arts and crafts, the beadwork, and that sort of thing?

A   I think that can be handled in a way so it would be something that would be of credit to the people, if it was handled differently. But I think we've got to keep it away from these Indian powwows and anything that builds up a strictly lot of this so-called Indian custom and culture that we hear them talk about it; it's not exactly true. A lot of it is farfetched and it's time to let it go by, because it has no value to it for the benefit of the people, for their uplift, and for the moral good.

Q   One thing that the Reorganization Act did was allow freedom of religion on the reservations; any religious body could come in, and it also let in the Native American Church.

A   That's right.

Q   Was that one of the reasons you opposed it?

A   Yes, it is. That's one of the important reasons. We have here on the Yankton Reservation—I believe that they have it on Rosebud and Pine Ridge, so I've heard anyway. I haven't attended many of their meetings, but I know we have it here on the Yankton Reservation—the use of peyote in this Native American Church. They use that as sort of a ritual, you know, and I think that works about the same as a drug, and it's a health-ruining drug, whatever it is. I've never tried any of it, but I know a lot of people; I can tell a peyote user as far as I can see him.

Q   What does it seem to do to them?

A   Well, if he was out there a hundred yards from me, my eyes are not any good any more, but if he was out there a hundred feet, I can tell whether he's using peyote or not, if I've known him before he got to using it. It changes his complexion, it changes his attitude, it changes his talk, and I've seen them so full of peyote they are actually not themselves.

Antoine Roubideaux

Brule Sioux

Rosebud Reservation, South Dakota
Interviewed by Joseph H. Cash
Summer 1967

Antoine Roubideaux has died since this interview. From 1934 on,
he was either tribal chairman or tribal secretary and the longest
continual employee of his tribe. He was in his seventies at the
time of this interview.

ANTOINE ROUBIDEAUX Congress passed this 1934 act. And the only
way they go into effect would be to have the tribe ratify it—whether they
want to go under it or not. And the Government—Mr. John Collier who was
Commissioner of Indian Affairs at that time—called me into Washington. I
was just a rancher and a farmer at that time. Just a young farmer and
rancher, and I went into Washington. And they educated us, or gave us an
orientation, on this law. I came back and then started in with my people.
I talked to the people all over the reservation about it. The Government
paid the expenses. And the people voted and ratified to go under it. The
next step was to organize it. We had to set up a constitution and bylaws.
The old council at that time was just getting organized themselves, and
they've been operating for many years. I talked to the old council several
times about setting up a new tribal council under this section sixteen, under
a new constitution and bylaws, and I suggested to them that they set up a
constitutional committee. If they did, then they would be working with
them drafting the new constitution. And they did set it up, they appointed
five. They got the committee set up, but they didn't know which way, which
direction to go. W. O. Roberts was then the superintendent. He called me
in and suggested that it's possible that they'd like to have me lead off for
the committee. So we met several times. I met several times with the constitutional committee, and I suggested that we request John Collier, the

159

Commissioner of Indian Affairs, who was the guy that was really behind this 1934 act. He wanted to get the people organized so the Indian tribes would be self-governing people, handling their own affairs, controlling their own money, controlling their own land. Before that, the BIA was handling everything.

The tribe had money deposited here, but they couldn't spend it the way they wanted. If the old council passed a resolution wanting to use that money for a certain thing, the superintendent said no; well, that was it. They take that money and use it as they saw fit. So I met with the constitutional committee and asked them that we request legal help from the Interior Department, which we did, and the superintendent wrote the request for us. The constitutional committee signed it and sent it in to Washington. About two weeks later, two lawyers came out here—Felix Cohen and Fred Diker. We met for about a week straight with the committee, and they worked on this new constitution. The constitution that we operate under now—they worked on it. They got it all set up. I had to get out with the committee into every community of the reservation to explain it. They had to vote on it—yes or no. So we explained it to them and they voted on it. I think it was in November they voted on it. And it carried; they adopted the constitution.

Eugene Little, one of the long-hair Indians, was the chairman of this old council. He was opposed to ratifying under this 1934 act. He had great followers; they called themselves the old dealers. They're the ones that opposed everything—the referendum on the 1934 act, the constitution, and the charter. Well, they ratified the constitution. And the old council had faith in me, that's why they elected me as the first president. Right after the first year I got elected, I was called back into Washington and stayed in Washington thirty days on this charter. They drafted a charter.

JOSEPH H. CASH   What's the advantage to having a charter?

A   It gives you an opportunity to do business with the outside world —like, you know, making contracts and agreements, and like borrowing money, we had the power to borrow money.

Then they sent a man out here to work with me, His name was John Haggerty from the Blackfeet tribe. He and I worked together. We followed the same procedures we did on this constitution and bylaws. The Secretary of Interior set the date on March 16 that the people are going to vote now on this charter—yes or no. The same day they set a date for Pine Ridge, and Ben Reifel who is now a congressman, he was what they called an organizational field agent. They sent him out there, to Pine Ridge. So he worked out there. He's one of our members of this tribe; he worked out there and I worked here. We won here, but he lost it up there. So they put in a request again. The tribal council put in a request, you know, to have the Secretary of Interior authorize another election. Because the Government was paying all the expenses of these elections. So the request was made.

Frank Wilson was then the chairman of the tribal council out there, and he had the council put in a request that the Government assign me out there, and that the Government pay my expenses. So it went into Washington and came back down here to the superintendent and it was up to me if I take the job. They'd be willing to pay my expenses. So I talked the thing over with C. R. Whitlock. He sent the police out after me at my place, and I came in. He showed the letter to me and said, "Read that; it's up to you." So I read the letter. I asked him, "Now, you're my superintendent, and I had a lot of work in this organizational work. What is your advice?" "My advice would be to stay home, not go out there." And then the chairman of the tribal council came down here asking me if I would come out. I told him it's no use. They're defeated. They done a poor job in the first place and it's going to go that way again the second time, which it did. The second time it came up, they lost it again. But when our constitution was drafted here, ratified, then they took our copy of the constitution. Chairman Wilson came down and saw me; he talked to me. He said, "Well, how'd you go about drafting this?" "Well, you put in your request with the Secretary of Interior to send out a couple of his lawyers." And I gave them the names. So the council passed the resolution and they came out. And they worked with this committee. I think it was the first week in September, and they had a big fair out there. The superintendent sent the police out again, he wanted to see me. So I came in. He said, "I got a call from W. O. Roberts that I've got to deliver you to the Pine Ridge agency. They're working on this constitution, and they want you to talk to the people during their celebration." So I said, "Well, I'll do that, but I can only do it one day. If they want me to talk to the public, I'll talk to the public." So the police took me out there, out to Pine Ridge. I must have talked to about two, three hundred Indians there. I told them why they must organize. You need a definite organization constitution. You've got to have definite powers and authority. You've got to do business. That's the only way they'll do business with you. I talked to them in Indian. And when they voted on it, it went through. I went out to Kyle, I went out to Porcupine. I helped them out on this constitution . . . .

At that time, it was a new thing. You had to deal with laws and some of them were a little bit skeptical, they were afraid to move, see. But I finally moved them around and I got them started and got this charter ratified. And at that time, you know, the Depression was on. Everybody was hard up. And that's what I told my people. You're all hard up. I hate to see you walking out on the road, many times I pick some of you up on the road. You've got to get these things done. Your tribe could borrow money and you could go into the cattle business. You could farm your own land, develop your own resources. And that's what they did. And it's been going ever since then.

They set up over a period of two years about fourteen livestock associations. And at that time, the Rosebud Sioux tribe had a break. You know, during that time they were borrowing all these REA cattle. The Government brought up all these cattle. They had a bunch of them down in old Mexico. So John Collier writes to me and says, "If you want some cows, we'll give you some cows on repayment." In kind type of repayment, see. Instead of paying cash back, if they give you ten head, you pay back ten head, say in two or three years. So I accepted that, and I think they shipped us about three hundred head. And that's when we start putting out these cattle to the Indian people. And in addition to that, give them a cash loan.

They came out here with allotted sums of money, and they started developing these community irrigation gardens. Then they showed these Indians how to run these things. In addition, they built about eighteen or nineteen canning kitchens. You saw one here, the white building next to the arts and crafts building.

Then they got the Indians to get together and grow wheat. And the Government would go out there and thresh it for them. They bring the wheat in here, and they make flour, and they make pancake flour, and take it back out to them. Then the Indians had flour for the winter. That was a good program. It was operating smoothly until World War II broke out. Then they just jerked the program out.

At that time they had an extension woman here who went into about every community. And then they bought them pressure cookers and sealers and cans and everything they use to can their food, showed them how to do it. And the indivduals that had vegetables they wanted to can, well they bring it to this canning kitchen and they can their own food. And that was a good program. But the Government furnished the money, see, and they supervised it. And that's how the thing was a success. Of course, when World War II broke out, they just jerked out their money. And at that time, we had the CCC program, you know, where they were going around building dams and reforestation work. Today, if you see many dams on the reservation, they built them, the Government did. They must have put about three hundred Indians to work. If you had a team of horses that will pull a scraper, they put you to work. They had them in groups all over building dams. At the same time, they had a lot of rodent control work. You know, like the prairie dogs were overtaking the rangeland. They had a group working, going around poisoning them. And they built a lot of dams. The dams that we have on the reservation, the CCC built them.

Q   Tell me, Tony, did you notice any split here between the fullblood and the mixed-blood Indians?

A   We don't have that trouble here. They really work well together. Now you take Pine Ridge—Pine Ridge is really bad for that. It's about what I call discrimination.

Q   But none of it here?

A   The half-breeds don't discriminate against the full bloods, but it's the full bloods who discriminate against the breeds, because they have some white blood in them, see. And they feel that the breeds were getting all the benefits. Now once in a while somebody here on this reservation will mention that. But I talked to a lot of them about it—that they shouldn't feel that way. Because, after all, they're enrolled members of this tribe, I said, same as you. And you all have the same economic opportunities. The only thing that you must do is get in there; take advantage. Nobody is going to bring it to you. That's the way I talk to them. Now we don't have that trouble here.

Q Did that older element that went around the old treaty council continue to buck you during the thirties?

A Yes. What they called the old deal council. They tried to convince the people to vote no on this 1934 act. Same way with the constitution and same way with the charter. When they'd meet, there'd be about two or three hundred of them meeting. And they'd call me out there and tear me apart. They'd give me hell. But I stayed with them and for educational purposes, I kept telling them, "Your conditions and situations are bad." I said, "Let's get organized and get some help to your people, because you're old, you're old men, you can't farm, you can't ranch, and you can't go to college, and there're no economic advantages to you—but your children, your grandchildren need that help. Why do you try to block them from making progress? Well, I convinced some. They stepped out. But that group kept going, and kept going, and kept going. They went up to World War II, and then these old fellows started dying off. Finally they just went out. We don't have any more factions. But I really did put up a tough time in those times.

Steve Spotted Tail

Brule Sioux

Rosebud Reservation, South Dakota
Interviewed by Joseph H. Cash
Summer 1967

Mr. Spotted Tail, now deceased, was a World War I veteran, a
longtime leader at Rosebud, and a grandson of the famed Chief
Spotted Tail. He was seventy years old at the time of this interview.

JOSEPH H. CASH   Do you remember what happened during the thirties
when the Indian Reorganization Act came in?

STEVE SPOTTED TAIL   We had a general council they called it, before
this Indian Reorganization Act came up. And that's for the whole people.
And we had districts at that time instead of these communities. When the
reorganization started, we had these communities. But before that we were
in districts, like Parmalee district, and Rosebud, or Two Strike or whatever
—they were in districts at that time. There were some leaders in those
districts; they called them board of advisors or something like that. And
before this reorganization started, of course, there were some younger
people, and they had a little education, and they wanted to start this
Reorganization Act. And at that time I was a delegate to this general council. They had it in Parmalee at the Indian dance hall. And there was one
guy, he said if we do away with this general council and organize another
council, they were going to have this old gentleman who was chairman of
this council be chairman of this Reorganization Act. That's what they told
him. And they told him to sign some papers. He didn't want to do it for
quite a while, but it came along and he signed the papers. Well, they
organized and they left him out. He was an old man—Eugene Little they
used to call him. He was from Spring Creek. He was chairman of the general
council. When he signed those papers they all left and went back to
Rosebud, I guess. And they organized another meeting, not a council. And
they had a younger man as chairman. And they left him out.

Antoine Roubideaux

Brule Sioux

Rosebud Reservation, South Dakota
Interviewed by Joseph H. Cash
Summer 1967

Antoine Roubideaux has died since this interview. From 1934 on, he was either tribal chairman or tribal secretary and the longest continual employee of his tribe. He was in his seventies at the time of this interview.

JOSEPH H. CASH   I've heard that the Catholic Church opposed the Indian Reorganization Act. Is there anything to that?

ANTOINE ROUBIDEAUX   Yes. Not only the Catholic but the other denominations. Because they were in with the Bureau of Indian Affairs, you know; they controlled the lives of the Indian people. And they couldn't worship their own way or exercise their ceremonies. And that was one reason why Mr. Collier, the Commissioner [of Indian Affairs] at that time, said that they were denying their freedom of worship. And that's how what we call peyote started with the Native American Church.

The Bureau had, in conjunction with these various denominations, set up regulations. Like stopping Indians from growing long hair, stopping the Sun Dance or any other ceremonial dances, and by making sweat baths their own way. And they couldn't exercise any of their own culture. They got regulations set up so they could only dance Indian just once a month. And they had to get permission from the superintendent. These things were all set up in conjunction with these various denominations of churches. Mr. Collier came along and said, "No, you're denying the freedom of worship. Let the Indians exercise these traditions, cultural, any ceremony he wants like he used to. Leave him go." And that was the reason they knew that if the Indian people went under this 1934 act, they would lose control of the Indian, you know.

I heard one fellow talk to the old deal council out here, that it was a socialistic form of government that John Collier was trying to set up on this Indian reservation. It's an organization like across the ocean, he'd say. They had these Indian missionary workers working against it. They don't want the Indian to go back to the old days—the way they worship—they want to exercise their cultural heritage and ceremonies or whatever you call it. That was the reason why.

Today, the Indian exercises his worship the way he wants to. They could dance every day and every night if they want. They put on Sun Dances here, and what they call *yuwipi*—it's a ceremony where they bind them up with string and they talk to little spirits—and they could do that now.

Cecil Provost

Yankton Sioux

Marty Mission, South Dakota
Interviewed by Joseph H. Cash
Summer 1968

———————

Mr. Provost was business manager of Marty Mission and very
active in tribal politics. He was forty-seven years old at the time of
this interview.

———————

JOSEPH H. CASH   The people of the Yankton Reservation rejected the
Wheeler-Howard Act and have never gone under it. Do you happen to
know why this is?

CECIL PROVOST   It probably wouldn't have been rejected, but at the
time when the people were wanting to find out what this Wheeler-Howard
Act was all about, everything was hush hush. Nobody explained what it was.
And from a series of meetings they had trying to find out what this was all
about, the Commissioner of Indian Affairs, John Collier, came down and
was very much upset over the fact that the Indians are slow in adopting
this, when the other reservations have already gobbled it up. In the process
of interrogation, Collier was pretty much upset, and he said, "All right, boys,
tighten up your belts. You're going to get under the Indian Reorganization
Act whether you like it or not—you come crawling to us—we'll starve you to
death." So he did. John Collier starved us to death. And I was one of them.
I remember that, and I'll be darned if I'll ever get under the Indian
Reorganization Act as long as I live, for the fact that I was starved to death.

Q   Did he actually say that?

A   Yes, he did, at Greenwood, South Dakota, right there at the
meeting. That took place right at the time when the Depression was in full
swing. There was nothing. No rain; dust, grasshoppers—day after day. There
was nothing for anyone to make a livelihood on at that time. You couldn't
buy work even if you wanted work. Relief was handled by the Bureau of

Indian Affairs. Apparently, just from my own thinking, Collier must have stopped all this, because my dad and many others were refused relief. And for two weeks at a time, I had nothing to eat—just drank water, straight through. And I have never forgotten that to this very day.

And pretty soon the projects came about—the public works projects and the civil works projects. Again, the same ones were denied these works. At the very final stages of these projects, a bunch of them—my dad and many others—finally got on. They were building a road south of Dante, and a lot of them had walked as much as ten miles to get transportation to it. A lot of them worked at considerable distance. That was every day and night. And we were organized prior to that Wheeler-Howard Act—the 1932 constitutoin we had. But the Bureau also kept that under cover, saying we were unorganized, and they wanted to organize us into the Wheeler-Howard Act.

Q   You had your own constitution in 1932?

A   Yes. That was in force, in effect and approved by Commissioner Rhodes, I believe it was back in 1932. So it went on, and still it was the old fight. They still were determined to get us one way or the other. And over the period of years, it was always this group that was the favorite sons of the Bureau of Indian Affairs. It was just a handful. They got everything. They got all the benefits and everything. And the majority of them from that period on up to this day still haven't gotten any benefits of any kind except in commodities; that's about all they ever got.

Frank McKenzie

Brule Sioux

Milk's Camp, Rosebud Reservation, South Dakota
Interviewed by Joseph H. Cash
Summer 1968

———

Mr. McKenzie has been a long-time political and religious leader
of his people. He was in his late sixties at the time of this
interview.

———

JOSEPH H. CASH I understand there was an irrigation project down
here in the thirties. Do you remember anything about that?

FRANK MC KENZIE Yes, sir. To begin with, under the Wheeler-Howard
Act, they could organize a garden club and all that sort of stuff. And we took
advantage of this in our Milk's Camp here, and we had a nice Government
garden project here. And we got a nice dam not very far north of us here;
we irrigated our garden from this dam. And we sold something like over
$4,000 worth of canned vegetables to the Rosebud Boarding School. We sure
got a good benefit out of that. But later the Government took all their
equipment, canning equipment and everything. Well, then the garden
project died away, since that time.

Q When did they do that? Was that during the war?

A That was during, just about wartime.

Q Did the people cooperate and work together on this thing, do you
think?

A Yes. The people here all cooperate. I was chairman of the garden
club a couple of times. And the way we do, we work in the garden, and
every individual that puts in more time in working in the garden gets more
canned goods than the one that didn't put much time in. So those of us that
put a lot of time in the garden, we get a lot of canned vegetables. And
everybody got along fine. We had plenty to eat during the winter time with
our garden canned goods.

Cato Valandra

Brule Sioux

Rosebud Reservation, South Dakota
Interviewed by Joseph H. Cash
Summer 1967

Cato Valandra was formerly chairman of the Rosebud Sioux tribe
and a national officer of the National Congress of American
Indians. At present, he is president of Rosebud Electronics, Inc.,
and owns and manages a number of businesses on the Rosebud
Reservation. Mr. Valandra was forty-six years old at the time of
this interview.

CATO VALANDRA   I think the act of 1934, the IRA, was good, but I
don't think the Indian was really ready for it in 1934—education-wise,
managerial-wise. And it just took this process of getting people involved or
interested in tribal affairs because it was a dead proposition. And a lot of
other Indian reservations are in the same situation today; the drain-off of
potential leadership from reservations is terrific. Because what happens
when a guy goes out and gets a degree in business administration? There's
nothing here for him. There are elective offices; but you've got to go out and
continually campaign. My term of office here is two years. I've been in here
since 1954 but then not as chairman. I'll be going on my seventh year as
chairman, but I've been involved in tribal affairs since 1954. Quite by acci-
dent I got in. We're trying to get younger people involved. I talk to a lot of
young people all the time. When I say young, I mean fellows who are thirty,
thirty-five, forty years old, along in that group, twenty-five to forty. I try to
get them interested in tribal affairs. Your most successful farmers and
ranchers, Indian people, don't give a damn about coming into tribal politics
or tribal affairs, because they're happy where they are. They don't want to
become involved; so, as a result, they don't run. And in talking with these
people and trying to get them involved, you've got to form livestock associa-

tions for instance. That's a vehicle to get them involved. Then they become interested. Then you appear before them, talk to them about tribal affairs, and say, "Why aren't you people involved?" The better-educated, the progressive people. So that's what we're aiming for all the time. And over the years, in the last seven or eight years, we've gotten more of the young aggressive Indians coming into the tribal politics. It's beginning to show, because they're a more progressive group than they are with the older Indian who hasn't seen much change for the last hundred years or so here.

JOSEPH H. CASH   You're very active in tribal politics and you're now engaged in another campaign for office. How do you campaign?

A   I campaign the same way as any other politician does that's in a political battle. We form our committees, we have our people in the various districts who make periodic reports to us. We'll have a lot of people in this afternoon who see how things are—for instance, our Black Pipe Community, up in Ideal, or all over, see. You've got to have your people who are sympathetic to your administration working for you. And talking and the whole bit.

It's run a little bit differently than it would be on a state or national level. It's more or less the individual that they're going to vote for instead of an ideal government. So you have to project what you stand for, and what your platform is going to be to these people. They're primarily interested in what you can do for them, not what the results of some of the programs that you have will benefit them.

Q   Does the business of Democrat and Republican play any part?

A   No, it doesn't. It's really nonpartisan. These people don't vote on ideas of government or functions of government or how it should be run, a definite idea of how it should be run. There's no organized party here. I anticipate after the primary election is over and the two highest guys come out for the general election, then the two highest guys out of the vice-chairmanship come out, that there is a coalition of people on that thing. It might happen—I don't know.

Q   Does the Bureau play any part in tribal politics?

A   The Bureau doesn't; they can't afford to. They get accused of it. The Bureau gets accused of it. The churches get accused of it. Which is good political hay for someone who wants to go that way. But I have found that if I'm elected I've got to work with these people—the Bureau, the churches, the public health service, the school board, and everybody else— I've got to work with them. So if I kick them around during the election, I consider that kind of a negative approach anyway, because I think in order to win an election you've got to be positive about the whole thing. You've got to tell these people now, "You've got to get going here. You can't just be sitting on your fannies the rest of your lives waiting for the Black Hills claim to get in." So be positive about the whole thing. Tell them what to anticipate and what we'd like to do, and what we are doing.

Mabel Trudell

Santee Sioux

Santee, Nebraska
Interviewed by Herbert T. Hoover
August 12, 1970

Mrs. Trudell was seventy-four years old at the time of this
interview.

MABEL TRUDELL   I tell you, the Depression years were hard. It was
never like that before here—never again. Hard times—no jobs, no jobs anywhere. Farmers wouldn't hire anybody because they couldn't sell their hogs.
. . . Some of the people just didn't hardly have anything to eat. My husband
worked out for a farmer that lived close to us. He lived over by Center, and
he worked for this farmer. And he only paid him fifty cents a day. Mind you
he just worked for that. We had to make it with that.

The Red Cross came at Center and they helped the people. Toward
the last they give them orders. Like if somebody's got a big family, they give
them orders. Ten dollar order to take to the store to buy food. Until
Roosevelt got in there, and then the Government helped the Indians.

When Roosevelt came in, he fixed it so that the Government gave the
men jobs. Like they go to the white people and ask them if there was lots of
trees in the woods, and if the Indian men could go there and work. And then
the Government would pay them—they called it a purchase order. They
didn't give them cash. And they worked from Monday to Friday and they
got paid—wasn't very much. But that helped.

I think Roosevelt was a good man. I voted for him. There was a man
come and took us [probably in 1936]. He wanted who it was that was
running against Roosevelt at that time. This white man was for that guy. He
didn't want Roosevelt; he didn't want a Democrat. He was a Republican.
We were Democrats. But we didn't have a car, so he said he'd take us. We

172

had to go way out into the hills from where we lived, to a schoolhouse to vote. I never did vote. Never did. That was the first time. I told my husband. I said what I am going to do. "Well," he said, "the names and everything is on there, just so you vote for Democrats. Be sure and vote for Roosevelt." So this man took us. He wanted us to vote for his man—the one he wanted. We went with him. We both went in there and we both voted for Roosevelt. This guy didn't know it. We played a trick on him.

I said I'm a Democrat. And I will stay that way. I never voted for Republicans. I didn't say nothing at the time. But you know, a lot of white people were Republicans. That's when we had depression; we had a hard time. Some of these white people, farmers, had a hard time, too. They couldn't sell their stuff. They had a place in town at a store on the corner where they give all the people—Indian and white—clothes and food. And some of the men, the white Republicans, they go there and they get this stuff to eat—and clothes. And when Roosevelt run for three, or four terms, well then they didn't want him . . . . And all of these farmers that had a hard time, they wanted a Republican. They were voting for a Republican . . . . But Truman, I said I voted for him. I said, there are some people—I don't know what is wrong with them. Most of the Indians are Democrats. They always have been. After a Democrat president got in there, everything went good.

Today and tomorrow

Merri Pat Cuney

A Sioux Indian, Merri Pat Cuney is a senior at the University of South Dakota majoring in criminology. She plans to do graduate work in history.

Miss Cuney was raised in Rapid City, South Dakota, although her family comes from Pine Ridge Reservation where the Cuney Table, a geological area named for an ancestor, is located. The moccasins she wears to French class (opposite), were made by her grandmother, who remembers the Wounded Knee massacre. Merri Pat's grandfather is said to be one of the braves who buried Crazy Horse at a secret spot near Wounded Knee.

Miss Cuney talks with friends at the University of South Dakota cafeteria.

Extracurricular activities keep Merri Pat busy. She has taught at Pierre Indian School, tutored children at Sioux Falls, counseled at a drug program in Rapid City, counseled in prisons in Sioux Falls, taught Indian culture to a white Brownie troop, and was a delegate to Washington, D.C., for the Committee on Minority Problems. The Special Services Staff at the University of South Dakota discusses how to help Indian students adjust to campus life and succeed academically (opposite, top). Merri Pat jokes with her "gang" in downtown Vermillion (opposite, center). The Indian Research Project of the Institute of Indian Studies where Miss Cuney works part-time transcribing interviews for the American Indian (oral history) Research (opposite, bottom).

Indian House is an open social house for all Indian students. Miss Cuney arrived to find it showing signs of the previous evening's impromptu party. The broken screen door of Skin House—for Redskin—is the most obvious sign of all. Despite Randy Bordeaux's quip, "We can't fix the screen door. We'll lose our reservation status," Merri Pat, Angela, and Randy soon hinged the door back into place.

Miss Cuney also tutors second grade children at St. Paul's Indian Mission School in Marty, South Dakota. In her volunteer work with Indian children, Merri Pat found their severe shyness and English language difficulties the greatest obstacles to overcome.

Lehman Brightman

Oglala Sioux

Talk Given at University of South Dakota
Vermillion, South Dakota
February 1970

Mr. Brightman is editor of the *Warpath*, president of United Native
Americans, and a lecturer at the University of California. He is
recognized as one of the leading "militant" Indian spokesmen
in the United States. He was in his thirties at the time of this
interview.

LEHMAN BRIGHTMAN   When I started at the University of California
a couple of years ago, I was the only Indian graduate student in the University out of twenty-eight thousand students. And this is considered the leading
university in the United States today. And they had one Indian graduate
student, myself; and there was one Indian undergraduate student, a girl.
She belonged to my organization—the United Native Americans—and we
went over and talked to the Educational Opportunity Program and asked
them why they didn't have more Indians there. And they couldn't give us
a satisfactory explanation, so we told them we wanted some Indians in. They
have over one hundred thousand Indians in California alone. They agreed
that they would let us go out and recruit ten Indians and bring them in.
We went to work and brought in ten, and then we told them we wanted to
bring in ten more, so they let us bring in ten more spring quarter. That gave
us twenty, and we brought about two or three in over the summer. Two
dropped out, and we had discomfort here and there. And then this quarter,
this winter, we added thirty more people. So we have close to sixty. There
are six courses that are offered. We've got approximately forty students in
each class. We've got bigger classes than other ethnic studies departments
have and yet we have been underfunded.

Cato Valandra

Brule Sioux

Rosebud Reservation, South Dakota
Interviewed by Joseph H. Cash
Summer 1967

———————

Mr. Valandra was formerly chairman of the Rosebud Sioux tribe
and a national officer of the National Congress of American
Indians. At present, he is president of Rosebud Electronics, Inc.,
and owns and manages a number of businesses on the Rosebud
Reservation. Mr. Valandra was forty-six years old at the time of
this interview.

———————

CATO VALANDRA   We found when I came into office in 1954 that the
activities of the tribe were not known. In 1954, we came into office here
and took a look at it. There was only one tribal employee, paid directly by
the tribal council. For the amount of assets that the tribe had, why wasn't
something being done to improve, to accelerate some of the programs the
tribe had—the low rent on land, for instance, of $42 per quarter annually? I
don't know why. So we started increasing rental rates to conform to what
is being paid for non-Indian land in surrounding areas around the reservation and found that prices were depressed on the reservations. Why was it?
There shouldn't be any reason for it. Now this tribe is organized under the
IRA Act. It has a charter and a constitution that was adopted by these people
in 1934 and 1935. And the authority for creating additional income for the
tribe is contained in our constitution. We could determine that the Bureau
of Indian Affairs has more or less taken hold of the reins as far as the tribe
was concerned and was administering tribal affairs and leasing tribal land.
And without any real concern of the officials of the tribe about increasing
land rentals and promoting some tribal programs, because the Bureau of
Indian Affairs more or less had the whole picture.

JOSEPH H. CASH   Could you tell me the advantage of having the corporate charter? Pine Ridge doesn't have it.

A   Right. Pine Ridge doesn't have it. On the corporate charter, we could go to private lending agencies. We don't have to depend too much on the Bureau of Indian Affairs Revolving Credit Loan Fund. It's always broke anyway. There's never any money in there. You know, you go in there and apply for money and they tell you, "Fine, submit the application." And then there's never any money for lending purposes for the tribe; the funds are always depleted. So under our charter we have the authority to go out into the private sector—private sources, companies, banks and make loans. We're restricted to a limitation of what we can do without secretarial approval, for instance. Our charter says we can go out and borrow up to $75,000 without secretarial approval but at the same time if we want to borrow some money to buy additional land and we have an opportunity to borrow a half a million dollars or so, we have to go to the Secretary of Interior in order to do this.

Q   Have you done this?

A   We're in the process of doing this now. We have a meeting scheduled in Minneapolis Friday with an insurance company. I've been to the Secretary of Interior's office, and gotten his approval. And we've got the proposal written up, and we'll package it up and send it to him and see what he says about it. We think that the corporate charter of a tribe has a lot of authority in it. But it's a restrictive authority. We can only go so far. To give you an example of some of the things we can do, it says we can go ahead and purchase and take by gift, bequest, or otherwise hold, manage, operate, and dispose property of every description, real and personal property subject to these limitations: no sale, mortgage, or lease may be made by the tribe of any land except what is going to be held by the tribe, now and hereafter held by the tribe, except as authorized by law, the regulation of the Secretary of Interior, and the constitution of the tribe. Well, there's a restriction. No sale, mortgage, or lease may be made as a restriction. We have a limitation—a lease can't be any longer than ten years, with the exception of industrial leases. We have a whole list of restrictions. We have made some amendments to the charter since I've been in office here, since 1962, and we've amended and had approval from the Secretary of Interior. All the people voted on them and we have had some changes in both the charter and constitution.

Q   Have you run up against opposition from the Bureau of Indian Affairs in taking charge more of yourselves?

A   They have not actively opposed us. We have got along really well with the Bureau. The reason is we have more or less been in the same boat. We have included the Bureau in every activity that the tribe has initiated here. We use the Bureau extensively here. When we have lease problems, we call the Bureau over. We say, "Okay come on over. Now you guys are the experts in this. You're the resource people. You're the people who are sent out here to give us advice on this." Because we don't know all things about Bureau regulations or what can be done as far as leases are concerned. We do the same thing with education, welfare, law and order, the whole bit. And as a result of this close cooperation between the tribe and the Bureau, we've been able to get a lot of things done here that otherwise we could not have done. We do the same thing with the Public Health Service, the County Extension Service, the local school boards—all these things are done. And we work under the assumption that we can get a lot more done.

I think that we have good cooperation. And as a result of this, we get more done. I've had meetings with people from Washington and the Aberdeen office, and the local office here. The Public Health Service had a meeting here this morning talking about the acceleration of water projects—development of wells in the community and water systems—along with our housing projects, and what the tribe's anticipated plans were for next year. So all these things have a direct bearing. Now if we were at odds with the Public Health Service, they would probably not be coming down here to visit me and some of the people who work here. They would probably be sitting up there making plans for us that we wouldn't be involved in. So what we have to do is get together on all these things. And you can do it a lot more effectively by sitting across the table from one another and exchanging ideas and information.

Gerald One Feather

Oglala Sioux

Pine Ridge Reservation, South Dakota
Interviewed by Joseph H. Cash
Summer 1968

Mr. One Feather is presently the tribal chairman of the Oglala Sioux tribe. He was in his thirties at the time of this interview.

GERALD ONE FEATHER The democratic process hasn't really taken effect to a point where people really understand the democratic system. This might have some bearing on cultural leadership patterns. There are traditional leadership patterns that have been in existence, developed by your kinship structure. And the whole organizational concept is superimposed upon the kinship structure, and therefore, after some thirty years, they haven't stabilized yet.

JOSEPH H. CASH What exactly do you mean by the kinship structure?

A The kinship structure is a community. We call it *tiospaye*. It's a kinship that lives in a certain geographic area who are related by blood or through marriage. And it's still pretty much evident here. It's still the basis on which everything moves. I think that's why we have so much factionalism, because each group will probably—as far as they're concerned—be for themselves or the community. It's kind of a perpetual type of thing, rather than an organization that's moving with social change. I think we've had a lot of technological changes in the last several years, but the social change hasn't kept up with this.

Q They still hang tight to these kinship groups?

A They still pretty much operate on that level. In many areas, it's disintegrating. I mean, your basic kinship structure in some areas is dwindling; therefore, the organization might be ineffective right now. But, on the other hand, where the people are moving into the larger villages, there's no systematic social organization. The tribal government will supposedly represent the people.

189

Anonymous

Winnebago

Winnebago Reservation, Nebraska
Interviewed by Herbert T. Hoover
August 1970

This informant, a middle-aged resident of the Winnebago
Reservation, is kept anonymous to prevent personal discomfort,
as the interview dealt with contemporary politics.

ANONYMOUS   It was about ten years ago, a little longer maybe, that
we decided to organize and go to the school board. They were going to
have a caucus. We were going to try to get some of the Indians on the
board, and a couple of white people sort of sympathetic toward the Indian
people. We just quietly went around, promptly at eight o'clock. And the
first time we tried it, we got there and it was locked right after eight. Then
the caucus was over. So we started campaigning quietly; we got twenty-four
people that we knew we could definitely count on to vote for these people.
But we got up there, and they beat us right on the floor. They said, "Well,
everything's going to go by parliamentary procedure. First you address the
Chair." None of us ever heard anything like that, but we decided we were
going to abide by their rules.

There were just eight people holding office up there. There was about
sixty white people there. And there was just twenty-four of us. And so they
put three names up there, and they went on down, and we got voted out
every time.

Finally we had our last chance—one more position to be filled. I
scooted down the seats, and told them [the Indians] "Don't vote for anybody
else. Just vote for one man." So we tried it, and he got twenty-four votes.
But the others still beat us.

Then we got in on a write-in the next year. We went from house to
house, and told them what had happened at the caucus. So the next year we

got them in on a write-in. All the Indian people went. We typed the names out, on little strips, and handed them out. We went house to house again. That's how they got in the school board. But before that we couldn't get our big toe in there. We have five now. That's pretty good. And the other new school board members are understanding—more so than before. They were sort of biased. They had served on the board for years, so they weren't about to give an inch. The Indian people were down, they didn't have any voice on the board.

Now with the new school board we have these teachers' corps and they were quite interested. We had a man in art who introduced a lot of Indian art. The music, too, we had this year—an Indian woman sang an Indian lullaby. The students all learned it, and sang it. And I think some of the students associated themselves with the Indian culture they have been forbidden. Their parents, too, when they went to the mission schools, were forbidden to talk Indian or anything. So a lot of our people don't really know too much of their Indian culture. But the children want this type of education.

With the Bureau of Indian Affairs, we got funds to hire Dr. Howard, out of Vermillion—James Howard—to come down and teach the history of the Winnebagos to the people. And it was amazing, we never had less than eighty people there. The town hall was full all the time. He was real interesting. He had, let's see, about six sessions. People would kind of plan a menu, and then everybody brought a little something. Some would bring dessert and some would bring meat dishes, and like that, soup. Dr. Howard was real interesting. We told him, "We don't want you to lecture, standing behind a podium or something. Just sit down and talk like Indian people did." And it worked. That's the type of instruction that we would like to give the kids at school, but we haven't really found anybody that well-versed in Indian culture. Some of our people were approached to teach the language and how to write the language. So they might get that off the ground.

When Dr. Howard was giving these lectures, quite a few white people came, and the ones that came are the ones that surprised me, really. I thought they were the ones who were least interested. They came faithfully there every time. There is a lot of interest when it all is taught in the proper way. He just told facts and told how they came down here from Wisconsin to here. He gave that history, and a lot of their customs. A lot of our own people don't know why they wear eagle feathers.

Anonymous

Mdewakanton Sioux

Prairie Island Indian Community, Minnesota
Interviewed by Herbert T. Hoover
June 23, 1970

This informant is anonymous because Prairie Island and Red Wing, Minnesota, are small communities, situated close together, and personal relationships might suffer as a result of this candid tale of prejudice.

ANONYMOUS It is hard being an Indian person, so much harder when you work in shops and construction sites. How hard it is to advance. Say your supervisor or somebody you work with maybe had come in contact with Indians and had a bad experience. You probably had never seen them before, but because you are Indian, he might take it out on you. He won't come right out and say so; he wouldn't make it hard for you, directly, but he probably would make it harder for you to advance. I think this is one of the biggest problems that the Indians have today, no matter where they go. Because of this thing, I think the Indians today have a tough time trying to obtain and secure crafts in any field. It makes it that much harder for us to do.

I think it is harder in a smaller community, because of the fact that there aren't too many [only about eighty on Prairie Island] . . . . I have lived here for years. I'll bet you a dime on a dollar that the people in Red Wing [nearby industrial city] . . . would have nothing to do with you. They wouldn't come out and visit you, or something on that order. It's changing—gradually and slowly, it's changing. I think within the next twenty years the American Indian will make great strides. But not now.

Another thing in a small community like this . . . the Indian is not aware of county politics. You know what I mean—like the town board—trying to run for town board or something like this to help improve his way. He's not aware of politics; I would say ninety percent, maybe ninety-five percent of the people aren't aware of politics. . . . Like I say, within ten to twenty years from now, I think they will be participating more in it. They are just starting to be aware of it now.

There is a sort of tight knit family that runs the town and the county politics. If you are not married to a certain relative—sure, they will give you the job, but it's something that no one else wants. From there, to advance, well, you'll never make it in a million years.

Take the carpentry business here, it is a real good trade. There are quite a few young [Indian] people here that I think can make it. But yet, I don't see that local labor organization coming out here or getting in contact with somebody that knows a little something about this thing. If you have some possibilities, maybe he'll take him on as an apprentice or something. But you look up in the rolls, and I bet you won't find an American Indian among them—bricklayers, carpenters, plumbers, nothing. My neighbor here is a licensed electrician, but he never got it here. He had to go someplace else.

I could never get credit in Red Wing. I couldn't get a nickel. In Hastings, I guess they just take you for what you are. They say, "Well, heck, he shows that he is holding down a job and working. What the heck. He needs a car, he needs a TV, a piano, whatever he needs." That's how it starts, you know. You're just another person to them. Here [in Red Wing] it seems like whenever you walk down the street everybody looks at you. You can feel it.

I associate with everybody. But I find out nine times out of ten that the people I associate with around here just say hello and goodbye, and that's about it. Other people take a sincere interest in you. Not everybody, but some of them do. Like this year, I've been getting along. In general, it's not the rule. [Some of our Indian boys] came out of the service in the 1950s, who were in the air police. They came out, and there were job openings in the Red Wing Police Department. They applied for them, and they said, "No, you boys are just fresh out," they said, "You've got to be living here a while." A few months later, somebody that didn't even finish high school was on the police force. These guys finished high school; they went to the service right afterwards. So they had to go someplace else. I mean, this is the thing that I'm getting at. I don't think people should get violent about it, or have to demonstrate or anything. But the fact still remains that that's how it is. If a good book ever comes out about it, and people read it, I think they'd understand more clearly what the Indian has to face today . . . . The metropolitan areas are probably the best bet for an Indian, because the next door neighbor probably doesn't care what you are, or who you are.

Merri Pat Cuney

Oglala Sioux

Vermillion, South Dakota
Interviewed by Ramon I. Harris
December 1970

Miss Cuney is a senior at the University of South Dakota and
has been very active in campus Indian activities. She was
twenty-three years old at the time of this interview.

MERRI PAT CUNEY   I worked for the Pierre Indian School for two summers—my freshman and my sophomore summers—I was a counselor. They
brought in probably one hundred Indian kids; they are all state wards,
taken away from their parents. They live there year-round. About four or
five years ago, they conceived that they would take the kids [approximately
fifty of them] to the Black Hills, stay in Spearfish at the college [Black
Hills State College], and they'd make it a summer—just like a vacation a
family would have. They have maybe one counselor for five children, and
we'd be like their parents, and we did their washing. We disciplined them,
and we all went places and did things, and it was supposed to be a real
good thing for them.

The first summer I came, these kids were really ashamed of being
Indian. I can remember three or four times, kids going by in cars and saying, "Oh, look at the squaws," and the kids would take it so hard, and they
would say, "Oh, I think we're Indian," and I'd say, "Don't feel bad about it
because they are just ignorant. These people don't know what they are
doing."

We went to Mount Rushmore at the end of the summer, and the kids
were all shook up because they were going to see a real-live Indian—half
of these kids were full bloods and didn't realize it. They got to see the Indian
and talk to the Indian. He'd say, "What reservation are you from?" and

they'd tell him, but they couldn't see that they were one of his. That year they offered Indian psychology to the kids and then they came the next year. They were completely different kids. They weren't ashamed of anything. It was so funny—I had a couple of the same kids, and the same things happened with the kids going by and yelling "squaw." They said, "I'm glad I'm an Indian, we're going to go up and see that Indian that's just like us." That's the difference it made for that one year for those kids, you know. If they could get readers and psychology and science and all of this on their level; I mean you can work it in, but work in theirs as a proud heritage.

Q   It is a proud heritage.

A   Yes, but it hasn't been. Normally, when you think of an Indian, it's drunken Indian—it's got a very bad connotation. If someone says, "Hey you Indian," the first thing I'm going to do is I'm going to turn around and hit them, because I'm going to think you're thinking bad. I think they should teach the Indian language, and make these kids start talking it, but it's all so new. I think people are finally wising up to the fact that you're just not going to suppress the Indians. They've tried too long, and they are still here—and I think everybody is finally becoming proud of what they are. People are looking in history books to find out what they are so they can be proud of it. And we're lucky because we know what we are.

Lucille Childs

Mdewakanton Sioux

Prairie Island Indian Community, Minnesota
Interviewed by Herbert T. Hoover
June 11, 1970

———————

Mrs. Childs received her high school diploma in 1970, by taking a general equivalent development course, and went to work as an assistant librarian in a nearby public school. She was in her forties at the time of this interview.

———————

LUCILLE CHILDS   When I was small I lived here with my folks. Then I stayed with my grandmother—I lived there most of the time. There was my brother Tom, and my sister, Ann. We were raised mostly with them. We lived in Granite Falls, and Shakopee, and Savage, all around there. They were always moving here and there. After they passed away, I came back here. I was about nine years old when I first went to school . . . .

I went to day school [for one year]. And from there, I went to Pipestone and finished the ninth year, and I then went to Flandreau for two years . . . . I liked Flandreau, because there was more freedom there. At Pipestone, they were so strict. They marched, and for everything we had to be on time. There we had military training. That's mostly what it was. But at Flandreau you had a little more freedom. They weren't so strict. I liked it there, but I didn't finish . . . .

After I got out of Flandreau I went to work. I worked in Chicago and in Milwaukee. That's where I got married. I lived there ten years. I went to work there in 1939, and then we moved out here in 1950. All I did was take care of kids. My husband was an auto repairman. He worked different places—the auto shops in Milwaukee. Now he is with International Harvester. But I've been down here since 1950, for twenty years with the kids . . . .

196

And I just got through the general equivalent development class in Zumbrota. To this day, I don't know if I passed it or not. This is for adults that haven't finished school. You have to be over nineteen to qualify for that. At first, I think there were twelve or thirteen of us that started. In the end, when we took the exams, there were four of us. We had the English teacher and the math teacher from the Zumbrota school. We had to go to Zumbrota on Mondays and Thursdays for two hours each night. We studied grammar, literature; and we had two math teachers, one for each class. We went for ten weeks. We took our exams last week. I guess some of them failed one subject, but they can go back in July. The man that gave us the test said he will help them get through. Some of them can go back, and the ones that didn't go to Rochester to get their tests can go in September . . . . We had good attendance almost every time. The Indians made a good effort to show up every time.

My family has been going to school right along. I never had to force them to go to school. They always liked to go to school. I have heard that some have poor attendance. I suppose you have to look at the family situation. And I think the teachers try to put a lot of pressure on the children if they don't get their work done. I guess they kind of get after them in the classroom and they feel embarrassed. My kids never complain about anything like that when they come home. There was an instance where the teacher called one of my boys, "Chief Wooden Head," and after that the kids started calling him "Chief" and he didn't like that name. I suppose they do that to other Indian kids, too. And some can't stand that, when they tease them . . . .

I have four girls and four boys . . . . My daughter, Ramona, went to college. She was a good student in high school. She went to college at Winona State, for her B.A. Then she worked and taught school. And she went to school at the same time, and she got her Master's—in Chicago. She teaches there, and goes to school right there at the same college where she got her degrees. She's working on her Ph.D. . . .

My oldest boy went to Rochester Junior College and took electrical engineering there. Then he went to Dunwoody and finished his other two years there. He is working for Sears, the Auto Department at Knollwood Plaza, in St. Louis Park. Danny is in the Navy—he just finished in 1967, and wasn't going to college. He decided to serve his time in the Navy—he signed up for six years. He is in the Philippines . . . and he's a machinist, in maintenance, whatever that is.

Then I have a daughter in California. She's a housewife, and she's got two little girls. Then, Rita finished school in 1968, and she wanted to go to college . . . . She is going to enroll at the University of Colorado . . . . Dale was just telling me that he wants to take up machinist work when he gets through school. He's really interested in that . . . . All my children thought there was no use hanging around the reservation; there is nothing to do. The

BIA has been helping them. The BIA gives so much, and then the state helps; it's mostly from the state, I think. State grants are eighty percent, or something like that, for the Indian kids that want to go to school.

Q   Do you speak Indian in your home?

A   Oh, once in a while I do, when I talk to my mother or something like that. I don't speak too well. I can't pronounce some of the words. When I went to Indian school, we didn't have that—I mean we weren't supposed to speak in Indian.

Q   I understand you do beadwork in your spare time.

A   Yes, but I haven't done too much. I've been doing this and that—I take a lot of orders, but I can't fill them right along. It takes a lot of time to do it. When I was at Flandreau I took up the creative arts for two years. You had to do that—make your own designs and study those symbols, and all of that. I usually sell to Indian people that come looking for it.

Lehman Brightman

Oglala Sioux

Talk Given at University of South Dakota
Vermillion, South Dakota
February 1970

———————

Mr. Brightman is editor of the *Warpath,* president of United Native
Americans, and a lecturer at the University of California. He is
recognized as one of the leading "militant" Indian spokesmen
in the United States. He was in his thirties at the time of this
interview.

———————

LEHMAN BRIGHTMAN   The Bureau of Indian Affairs is the purest form
of colonialism in the world. Colonialism is where an outside force or government comes in and takes over the function of a group of people, such as the
Bureau of Indian Affairs has done with the Indian people. And they direct
our lives, our health, education, and welfare. All these white people that are
employed as superintendents, assistant superintendents, and what-have-you,
who direct our reservations. It's called colonialism, and that's what it is—a
pure form of it. We don't control any facet of our lives.

The Bureau of Indian Affairs, HEW, the Federal Government, they
even tell how many cattle you can raise on your land, how much timber you
can cut, how much hay you can cut, who you can lease your land to, how
much you can lease it for. Well, hell, this is our land, we should be able to
do with it as we please. And these are some things that need to be straight-
ened out. And I don't hate white people—I talk about them a lot; I hate
what white people have done to Indians. But I realize that there are good
whites and bad whites; but for every white man you see helping an Indian,
you'll find ten more over here cutting them down and stabbing them in the
back, and you find a lot of Indians cutting other Indians down too. You
know, by cutting each other down, we're not going to ever get anyplace;
we're going to have to help each other. And I'm not advocating violence,

I'm just saying that it's time we did something about some of the conditions that exist on our reservations.

Did you read in the paper the other day, in Gallup, New Mexico—Gallup, New Mexico, is a city that has existed on Indians alone for the last hundred years or more. They buy Indian products for little or nothing and sell them for about ten times what they paid for them. And they hold an Indian Centennial every year, and they invite tourists from all over the world to come there, and they make thousands of dollars. And they make all this money off those Indian people, and they give nothing in return.

The city of Gallup is really up in arms. The health authorities made them stop arresting approximately two hundred Indian people a night on a weekend. Two hundred Indian people—they put these into those jails. The capacity should be sixty and they put approximately two hundred in them. Men and women together are just thrown in, and they're complaining. The sheriff said it was a catastrophe. Where are they going to put all of these Indian people? They can't arrest them any more because they can only put sixty in. Well, they have been making their living by exploiting Indians for years. They even produce a cheap sort of wine there which they poison our people with. Why in the hell don't they put up something constructive like a cultural center, an alcoholic clinic? Why don't they set up something for our Indian youth so they have someplace to go? Scholarship funds for our Indian youth—they have been exploiting us for years. These are constructive things you can do. So we're going to pull a boycott against them, and we're going to do it this summer. I was just talking to some people last night, some Navajos, and they're going to get their people aroused down there. And they are going to pull a boycott, and we're going to invite Indian people from all over to take part.

John Saul

Yanktonais Sioux

Crow Creek Reservation, South Dakota
Interviewed by Joseph H. Cash
Summer 1968

Mr. Saul, a Hunkpati, is noted for his many contributions to Indian art. He was ninety-one years old at the time of this interview.

JOHN SAUL   Instead of living on my own allotment as the treaty calls for, here I am. Of course, I'm an old man now, but younger generations can have their homes on their allotment just the same as white people. When you come back into the reservation here, you see no windmill, no farm, no place. I've known different superintendents that have been in charge of this reservation. There was one good man, Major Chamberlain—he was a super-intendent, and he's the one man that didn't sit in the office. He put his overalls on, and got out among the reservations and worked. If you'd go to some place, and if the man is trying to do something like the Government wants, he'd pitch right in and help. I've seen him pitch hay for an Indian. I've seen him chop wood for log houses, and he issued two thousand head of heifers, issued two to each enrollment, and he cut the cottonwood timber and made lumber out of it. Out of the lumber, he had 150 homes built. Before that we were living in log houses, no floors, and tipis, on the reserva-tion, and that isn't very long ago.

JOSEPH H. CASH   Did you ever live in a tipi?

A   I was born in a tipi. Yes, sir, I'm passing ninety years old now, and I remember quite a way back. Before that lumber was cut and put into little frame houses instead of log houses—he issued 150, and I got one and built it myself. I know how to do carpenter work, and I built the house myself without help. Every place I look now in different homes, instead of the log house there's a little frame house with a floor in it.

Today, we're not able to have a home, a farm like the white people. Instead of having a farm out on our allotment, you see what they're doing here. All these buildings, they've been here, they're going to put us Indians all together, and we can't get out and raise cattle—nothing! We can't raise wheat or cotton. We can't do anything here, only pay the rent and live here, and that's all. Of course, I'm not able to work, but when I was a younger man, I did pretty good. The Government issued me two heifers, my wife two heifers, that's four. And she got issued horses, a team, and I had a team.

Now today when I sit here and compare with my time, I don't know what to think of this younger generation. What is the Government doing here? Why don't they put us on our allotment? Of course, we haven't got hardly any allotment, though I've still got land yet. I've still got a good 160 acres with that good spring on there. But I'm not able to have a home now, I can't get out and work like I ought to, but I've got grandchildren here, like this one here, and another one. I willed that land to them, and if they want to, they can use that land as they want. But I think that the Government has made a mistake when they put the Indians all together in one-half a section here. But what are we going to do? We're going to become showmen, that's what we're going to do. Tourists come around and make fun of us. By golly, we have the full American people here. This is our land, and the white people come in across the river, across the ocean, and start up the government here. I'm proud of them for what they did. But sometimes, I think they get too smart. Now they are trying to go to the moon to see if there's any Indian reservation up there.

Johnson Holy Rock

Oglala Sioux

Pine Ridge Reservation, South Dakota
Interviewed by Joseph H. Cash
Summer 1967

———————

Mr. Holy Rock was the tribal chairman of the Oglala Sioux tribe
and in his forties at the time he was interviewed.

———————

JOSEPH H. CASH   What about the Indians that move to places like
Rapid City? That looks like it's one hundred percent worse than living on
the reservation. Why go there? Why stay there under those conditions?

JOHNSON HOLY ROCK   I think the only reason they go up there is because of the lack of job opportunities at home. Since we've had OEO [Office
of Economic Opportunity] here, and there have been component projects
and work opportunities, there has been a tendency for them to drift back to
the reservation. It's not because they wanted to go over there but because
they had to. Economic pressure, no work opportunity, no earning power.
They figure that if they go to the centers of employment, that there's a lot
better chance of existing. I think that's the only reason we have Sioux
additions . . . because of economic pressure.

Q   Do you think they are better off economically in those places?

A   No, I don't think so. I've had occasion to look over the Sioux addition [in Rapid City] and I was appalled at what I saw. They're able to exist
there because they are used to a lower standard of living, and they have
not yet learned how to elevate their standards and improve themselves
generally over all. For many of them perhaps it is temporary. They're only
there because of work opportunities. Eventually they plan to come back to
the reservation. A lot of them do this off and on. During the summers they
work construction jobs of all types and when that's over they come back to
the reservation. And then because we don't have the work opportunity here

to take care of them, they're either on welfare assistance, or we have to increase our commodity assistance for food and what-have-you. Although many, many of them live in areas that are isolated on the reservation and lack work opportunity, I think they're a lot better off in many respects than living in a place such as the Sioux addition.

Gerald One Feather

Oglala Sioux

Pine Ridge Reservation, South Dakota
Interviewed by Joseph H. Cash
Summer 1968

Mr. One Feather is presently the tribal chairman of the Oglala
Sioux tribe. He was in his thirties at the time of this interview.

JOSEPH H. CASH   Do you think the Indian is being better educated
than he was?

GERALD ONE FEATHER   Well, I think he is. I know the younger generation's got more opportunities for education and more opportunity to go on
to higher education.

Q   How did you do it? How did you get educated?

A   I don't know how I got educated. It's a good question. I decided
to try college—this was my idea. I was never exposed to, or told anything
about, college life. I had to work for most of my schooling, I had to work
for it. I worked part-time to pay for most of my expenses.

I went to several colleges. I went to Dakota Wesleyan University in
Mitchell my freshman year. Then I transferred over to the University of
South Dakota where I got my degree. I did my graduate work at the
University of Oklahoma.

Q   You went to high school and grade school here?

A   Yes, I went to high school here. But since 1960, the educational
opportunities are more available, and funds to go with it are increasing,
which was never true before 1960. So I think since 1960 there's more opportunity for higher education because the funds are more available.

Q   Are there more kids taking advantage of it? Are they starting to
move now?

A   Yes, there are more of them.

Q When they get educated, do many of them come back here? Is there anything for them to do here?

A I think that's the whole trouble. Our economy development here hasn't reached a point where we can absorb all our educated people.

Johnson Holy Rock

Oglala Sioux

Pine Ridge Reservation, South Dakota
Interviewed by Joseph H. Cash
Summer 1967

———

Mr. Holy Rock was the tribal chairman of the Oglala Sioux tribe
and in his forties at the time he was interviewed.

———

JOSEPH H. CASH   Are you hopeful about your people?

JOHNSON HOLY ROCK   I'm very optimistic. I've always had confidence
in the people to help themselves, but the opportunity with which to help
themselves has been given and taken away from us so many times. I've seen
it over the years. In the beginning, when they issued cattle and horses as
they set up the reservation, there were no allotments. There were thousands
of cattle—Indian-owned. And they used to have great big roundups all over
the areas of the reservation. Each district had their own roundup crew, and
the other roundup crews from the different districts also participated, making one big gigantic roundup crew or several of them. They used to round
up and brand cattle for people who had cattle. My father had stock at that
time; sometimes they'd find some of his cattle up there near the badlands or
sometimes they'd find them down here in the sand hills of Bennett County.
It was all open country. The only thing that kept them in here was the
reservation fence. And they had a crew that went around and maintained
that fence. And any one of those old Indians with braids could go to the
bank and borrow money. The bankers in those days, they lent them the
money, regardless of what the statutes said or what the Secretary of
Interior's regulations were, they lent those old Indians money, and they got
paid.

When they shipped their cattle, they shipped two- three- four-year-old
steers. It was a booming economy. All of a sudden, they decided to make

207

allotments. They began to issue allotments—instead of letting the people remain as they were, they tried to make them individualistic. That was the worst thing they could have done. They were not used to this type of living. And then because ownership of property came into the picture, they began to separate the people, where before they had been operating collectively. Then the ones who got the allotments said, "Well, I think I'll just sell my stock." They began to bicker and quarrel among themselves because of property lines and so forth. Several of them went to Washington and said, "We want to lease our lands out. I don't like so-and-so using my land for nothing." So Washington said, "Okay, we'll lease your land out." So the Matador Cattle Company, one of the biggest cattle companies in the country, came in here and leased the whole reservation; and they stayed here I don't know how many years. When they left, they took their cattle and Indian cattle. There was no brand inspection in those days. Nobody kept brand books and nobody checked them out when they left, so they took their stock as well as the Indian stock, and that broke a lot of them. Then when the Reorganization Act started, they gave them replacement cattle. They began to increase the herds and they began to prosper. Then they came with the unit leases. They said, "Well, so many sections—only one person can make a living on this many sections. So we'll put out the unit system of leasing." It broke them again, those just beginning to get off the ground—it broke them flat. Many of them, they're still paying . . . off those replacement cattle. So it has been a matter of something like the game of "Button, button, who's got the button?" They give us an opportunity and we begin to advance; then they take it away and give us something else, depending on who happens to be in Washington and has an idea that should be put into effect, regardless of how it affects the people. That has nothing to do with it.

Lawrence Antoine

Brule Sioux

Rosebud Reservation, South Dakota
Interviewed by Joseph H. Cash
Summer 1967

Mr. Antoine was in his sixties when interviewed. He is writing a
book on the Rosebud country of South Dakota and is active in
church work and business activities.

JOSEPH H. CASH   Why does the educated class leave?

LAWRENCE ANTOINE   See where they're at. Like Dick MacKenzie and
all them guys who had a trade or any skill, well they left. There's nothing
here for them. No enterprise. I got two of my daughters in Denver now,
see. One of them is a nurse and the other one is just a nurse's aide. They
have to leave because there's nothing here. That's the same way with a lot
of this younger generation. So they're all moving into smaller towns so they
can gain employment. So what's left here are the ones that didn't finish
high school and had no incentive to go on. So that puts us, the reservation,
back thirty or forty years, the people that are left here. So you've got to have
a program to fit them. So we're a long ways from being ready to be turned
loose, I imagine you could put it that way.

Sam Writer

Ojibwa

Lake City, Minnesota
Interviewed by Herbert T. Hoover
July 14, 1970

Mr. Writer's life story is one of success through voluntary relocation. He was seventy-one years old at the time of this interview.

SAM WRITER   I was born and raised in Onigum. That's the reservation
there . . . . My mother died when I was two years old. My grandmother took
care of me then. And from then on we just lived from day to day in the
reservation. Let today take care of itself; tomorrow we'll do the same thing.
We never piled up the stuff we have got in the refrigerator and deep freeze
we have now—we didn't have those things many years ago. I often wonder
how we made a living. We cut wood for the Government. And Father would
cord the wood. And then we fished in the fall of the year. The white fish—
they would hang them up outside . . . so there were about seven or eight
hundred white fish. Outside—that was the deep freeze. From then, I found
out that there is no living on the reservation. You never have anything. It
was tax free. We could kill deer any time. We could set a net any time.
That's the way they lived. But I wanted to get away from that.

I went to school in Wahpeton, North Dakota. There are about twenty-
seven different tribes of Indians that go to school there. I used to run around
with a Sioux girl there. I talked that language, and they used to gad around
and laugh at me, you know, for how I pronounced those words . . . . I went
there from 1911 to 1915.

The year I got out of school at Wahpeton, that was in 1916, 1917, 1918
and 1919, I got in with the surveying for the Government. For three and a
half years I traveled thirty-seven states with them. I've been in Cuba and
Canada.

But after I got back, I knew there wasn't any future in the reservation. So I went to work at the Minnesota Steel Company in Duluth. And I saw a man shoveling snow out on the sidewalk, an old man. And it got me to thinking. You see yourself out there. You've got to get yourself to learn something. I was going to learn to be a machinist. But something sidetracked that, and I went to work—went on down and got a haircut in a real nice warm place. Those fellows wore nice, clean clothes. And I thought to myself, "I think I can save enough money and go to school in the spring," which I did. There is no future on the reservation . . . . I went back to the reservation for the time being, yes. Just enough to go to work, enough to learn at the barber school in the Twin Cities. I traveled all over . . . was a journeyman barber . . . an apprentice barber. I went to Milwaukee and got a job there. I worked in Stockholm, Sheboygan, and Fond du Lac. And what's the name of the town . . . Appleton, Wisconsin? Then I went to Green Bay, Oshkosh, and Kewaskum, Wisconsin.

I gathered a few things, just like when a person teaches you—go to some places and sit there and see what you can learn—what he does, the best part of the profession. And I learned quite a bit from them. And I went back to Milwaukee, Sheboygan, Kewaskum, and West Bend. And I just can't remember a lot of the other places that I've been. And finally, I went back to Minneapolis, and I read in the paper where they wanted a barber and a ball player in Medina, Wisconsin. That's her home [his wife] over here; that's where I met her. And I was there in 1927; and in 1928 we got married. And we've been here ever since. I enjoy it here.

I would encourage the young Indians and the young girls to get out and learn some profession, and they would be better off than if they would stick around the reservation. As I said, there's no future in it. Any of them will tell you that. As I said before . . . get off the reservation and learn something. Learn some profession—automobile mechanics, or go to barber school and learn that. The girls learn beauty-operating or nursing, or something like that.

They all respect you if you belong to some community. A lot of times they just knife you in the back. That I don't like. You've heard them. "Them damn Indians," and all this and that. I can't say anything bad about anybody. I never did. Oh, if I didn't like a person, I would say I didn't care about him. I don't hate him, but I just don't care about him . . . . Well, I've been here since 1927, and I have seen a lot of changes. One guy came into the Blue Moon Cafe one time when I was having coffee. Something had happened. He said, "They ought to give this damn country back to the damn Indians." "Oh, no, Mister," I said, "not with the debt you've put on it." And everybody went up with laughter . . . . We have had some trouble, but it didn't amount to very much.

Levi Lawrence

Santee Sioux

Santee Reservation, Nebraska
Interviewed by Herbert T. Hoover
August 11, 1970

Mr. Lawrence's life story is one of success through self-
improvement and voluntary relocation. Mrs. Lawrence was
also present and participated in the interview. Mr. Lawrence
was fifty-three years old at the time of this interview.

HERBERT HOOVER   How is this farm land around here? Is it very productive?

LEVI LAWRENCE   No, there isn't. The whites came in to farm the land.
around here.

Q   There isn't much reservation land left is there?

LEVI LAWRENCE   No, there isn't. The whites came in to farm the land.
I never did find out whether they leased the land or bought the land or
what—but there is quite a few farmers that are farming this land now.
Right at the present though I don't think that there is an Indian that is
farming, that I know of.

Q   There isn't an Indian farming!

MRS. LAWRENCE   Used to be.

Q   Do you folks get any income from leased land?

LEVI LAWRENCE   He lives on social security now [points to his father].

Q   Where do the young people go? The tribal chairman told me the
other day that when a young fella grows up now, he just leaves the reservation.

MRS. LAWRENCE   Lot of them go to Sioux City I think—to cities like
Sioux City and Omaha, Sioux Falls.

LEVI LAWRENCE   I know that I lived here in 1936. When I finished
here I went down to Haskell Institute, Lawrence, Kansas. I stayed there

five years. I took a trade, a printing trade. And I lived down there. I made my living on that the last twenty-five years. I don't work any more; I'm disabled. We lived in Lawrence a number of years. I worked for the daily paper there and then I lived in Pierre and worked for Hipple. From there I went to North Dakota—Wahpeton—and I went back to Lawrence again, back to the old place where I started. I was trying to work myself to where I could get more money. Because I was the only Indian with the group of sixty or seventy employees, I had to buck my way and fight to get what I can. I'm always looking out for better wages. If I see one, I usually try to apply for it. That's how I moved so much. From there in Kansas I went to Utah. Then we moved back to Rapid City. Then I got sick and I wasn't able to work; I was laid off of my job. I sold all the furniture and with necessary things we needed—I bought a trailer—we hightailed it for California. And I was out there about four years, and I found a job the week after I was there, and I was doing good there until I got sick again. Wages were good but the living was high.

Q   How old are you?

LEVI LAWRENCE   Fifty-three.

Q   Do you think you are fairly typical of the people that you grew up with? Most of them went away?

LEVI LAWRENCE   Most of the ones I used to run around with here. Some of them have passed on, and some of them lived in Sioux City and Omaha, big cities, you know. And their younger kids . . . when they go to the cities like Sioux City I imagine most of them work for the packing house. They take unskilled work. But with me, I was determined to get that trade, which I did, and that's helped me with the last twenty-five years.

MRS. LAWRENCE   It's always hard to get a decent salary though. Boy, we've gone through something.

LEVI LAWRENCE   I got kicked in the face, and called everything under the sun.

MRS. LAWRENCE   One time we lived in a furnished apartment, and I said, "Well, we've got to borrow furniture and get a house 'cause we've got a family now." And he went and wanted to borrow money so we could have a stove and a refrigerator. And that man told him, "Well, that's a luxury, you don't need that." Try and find a place to live. Well, a slum, you can find that, but you don't want it. You've really got to fight to get to live someplace else.

Q   Were you turned away from housing?

LEVI LAWRENCE   Oh, yes.

MRS. LAWRENCE   Told to go to hell.

Q   Where?

MRS. LAWRENCE   In Rapid City.

Q   Is that the worst you encountered?

MRS. LAWRENCE   Yes.

Q   What about California?

LEVI LAWRENCE   No problem; the only problem they had out there was with the Mexicans. For a while the people kind of looked at me as if I was one of them, you know. So after they found out that I was an Indian, then they were much more pleasant.

MRS. LAWRENCE   There were some prejudices out there, too. But not like Rapid City.

LEVI LAWRENCE   They're so down on Mexicans. Quite a few people out there are Mexicans, you know, and Puerto Ricans.

Q   How about Pierre?

MRS. LAWRENCE   That's not too good either.

LEVI LAWRENCE   We lived there, so we know. I imagine it's a little worse than what it was when we were first there. Yankton used to be good. I don't know how it is now. I went to school in Yankton, Central High. I went through eighth grade there; it was good. I got along good with all the kids I went to school with. But today, I don't know how it is. I haven't been back down there . . . .

Q   What do you recommend to your own children?

MRS. LAWRENCE   Get an education.

LEVI LAWRENCE   Education is one of the biggest things today. Just like our boy there; we try to tell him get all the education you can get and get along with your fellow man. Regardless of who they are. For me, when I first went and got on a job I was backward kind of. Don't say much, you know. But after I found out the way they were pushing me around, well then I was thinking I guess I'll start opening my mouth. The longer I worked with the white man, the more I caught on to his ways. A lot of times I felt like quitting real bad, but then I grit my teeth and go back at it again. But you just have to. I tell this to a lot of the Indian boys that I talk to, and a lot of them ask me how do I go about getting where I am. Well, I just tell them that I fought my way. Let the man know that I am just as equal, and just as smart and capable of doing the work that he's doing. In fact, I put out twice as much work as any white man that ever worked next to me, and yet I got the low wages. This is what I had to fight.

MRS. LAWRENCE   We had to work a lot of times in order to get that same salary that the white man gets; we've had to work twice as hard to show that we could do it, and that white man right next to you isn't doing half that work. But in order to get that salary and hold it, we had to do it that way.

LEVI LAWRENCE   But I proved it.

MRS. LAWRENCE   I think that's why he had a heart attack when he was forty years old. He's had two now.

LEVI LAWRENCE   I used to get so darned mad, but then I just made up my mind that I'm going to fight it, and fight it, and I go back the next day.

MRS. LAWRENCE   Of course, it's going to be slow. But people are more aware of Indians now, and some of these others growing up now, they might not have to fight like we had to.

LEVI LAWRENCE   I got so where I used to get into some heated arguments, you know. I used to say, "If you don't like it, there is the door, let's go outside." And that's where I got my experience, by working that way, finding out what the other fellow was like. I made some good friends though; I made some enemies too. But still the majority of them, I made good friends. That was my biggest point—to make friends. Then I figured sometime if I need help, if I am out of a job maybe I can go back to that shop again, I mean that's the way I look at it. That's how come I got back down to Lawrence and Wahpeton, got in pretty good with the big boss, and I asked him if he had an opening, and he said sure, he'd welcome me back. And that's the way I look at the job when I go out. Try and make friends and do the best I can in case I'm out of a job sometimes, I might want to come back to that old shop, you know. So I can say I achieved what I went after. I could have been still going, probably; sometimes I feel like going back.

Q   From what you say, Rapid City really has its problems.

MRS. LAWRENCE   Oh, have they ever!

LEVI LAWRENCE   They do. On both sides, the Indian and the white side. I'd say twenty percent are the ones that's causing all this trouble that goes on down the street, and in these bars, you know. But yet, they don't condemn the white side of it. They condemn the Indians—entire group— instead of just looking at the twenty percent that you see day in and day out. I mean that's all you see when you go up town. You see that same bunch of faces day in and day out. The rest of us very seldom go up town. The only time we go is if we need something. But yet we are condemned right along with them, and this is something that I myself disapproved of. I have got in arguments over it, try to prove to them that they were wrong. I say, "Why don't you condemn your own people that do the same thing?" They will overlook that. We get abused in some of the stores through the clerks.

MRS. LAWRENCE   We haven't been waited on. We will go in a store and not get waited on. They just leave you standing there.

LEVI LAWRENCE   But it's very few places that would do that now. If they get to know and see who you are, and know what you're doing, well then their attitudes change.

Q   Do you have problems getting credit?

LEVI LAWRENCE   It is rather hard. I experienced that, too. But of course now the majority of them there that do try to get credit of course are these type of persons that don't hold a job down, like they should, you know. They work so many days and ask for their pay and they take off for two, three days on a big binge. This sort of thing is what hurts them. I used to tell them if you've got a job, hang on to it until you get what you want, and try to improve yourself; and the more you improve yourself the better off you will be, and probably get more money as the time comes. The biggest starting point is to improve yourself. If you don't try to prove yourself, and if the boss sees that you're not trying to hold that job, naturally he's going to can you.

MRS. LAWRENCE   They say there are no jobs for Indians in Rapid unless it's dishwashing or something like that. Even if you've gone to school. They just don't get up in this other bracket, better jobs.

LEVI LAWRENCE   Even some of the restaurants. Some of these young Indian girls would like to be waitresses, and they wouldn't hire Indians.

MRS. LAWRENCE   They all had dishwashing jobs. Or lawn mowing for a man, you know.

LEVI LAWRENCE   It's altogether different today than when I went to school. I went to public school too, but that's been a long while.

Q   And it gets harder and harder for kids?

LEVI LAWRENCE   It is.

MRS. LAWRENCE   That's why I still say I think it's the parents. I don't know why parents should have changed all of a sudden. They are our age. My sister graduated from high school in Wagner, and there were four Indians graduated that year with her. It was a big class. And in the operetta, those four Indians had the leading roles out of choir singing, and the white kids were no problem. They just went along and everything was fine when we went to school. I went one year in Wagner. But now I couldn't send Bobbie to Wagner. They say it's just gotten terrible, and there's been Indians living in that town ever since I can remember. We were born there.

I went to business college in Rapid and it was nice when I went there. Nobody ever made any differences whether I was an Indian or not, and I stayed with a nice family. And they never hemmed and hawed around. I ate with them, and there was never no problems. And now the kids just have a terrible time—since World War II. I always say we got so many southerners up there in that air base, and, of course, they are that way, you know, down there with the coloreds. So they are that way wherever they go with minorities. Rapid City used to be a nice town. There were a lot of Indians living there when I went to business school there and they had jobs. There was never an Indian problem unless it's problems that they started on the reservation. Now there are no jobs. They are discouraged. They go to town and they still can't get one.

LEVI LAWRENCE   They throw that education thing at them, see. A lot of them, they are not educated. Of course, that is the biggest downfall.

Johnson Holy Rock

Oglala Sioux

Pine Ridge Reservation, South Dakota
Interviewed by Joseph H. Cash
Summer 1967

Mr. Holy Rock was tribal chairman of the Oglala Sioux and in his
forties at the time he was interviewed.

JOSEPH H. CASH   I've heard it said that there's a terrible split between
the fullblood Indian and the mixed-blood Indian. Do you agree with that
or not?

JOHNSON HOLY ROCK   There are problems between the two factions,
but when the chips are down, such as in the experience we had a few
years ago where the state was taking over criminal and civil jurisdiction
over the Indian reservations, then there was no full blood/mixed blood.
Ranks were closed, all in one common effort to defend themselves against
something which they felt was an encroachment on them without consulta-
tion. When that happened, there were no split ranks. Just like you would
have in the United States—you have your Democrats and your Republicans.
They fight tooth and nail, but when the national security is in jeopardy,
what happens? You don't differentiate between a Democrat and a Republican. They close ranks at once because they have a mutual interest, one
common cause. And the same thing happens here between the full blood
and the mixed blood. When something comes up of mutual concern, then
there's no division. But otherwise, they have their arguments—pro and
con—just like the political partisans in the United States.

Anonymous

Brule Sioux

Rosebud, South Dakota
Interviewed by Joseph H. Cash
March 1970

The informant, who wishes to remain anonymous, said to refer
to her as a "beautiful Sioux maiden," twenty-two years of age.
This tale would seem to indicate that while the hippie community
feels a great identity with Indians, the Indians aren't so sure.

ANONYMOUS   The hippies came to the reservation last summer in
tens and twenties and camped at Ghost Hawk Park. They took off all their
clothes—both men and women—and were skinny dipping and dancing
around down there.

JOSEPH H. CASH   Were they Indian dancing?

A   I've never seen any Indians dance like that. But I suppose they
were doing what they thought was Indian dancing.

Q   Were any of the Indians dancing with them?

A   No. We were all in the bushes and trees with cameras taking
pictures. We'd never seen anything quite like that.

Q   Then what happened?

A   The tribal police came and arrested them and took them away.

218

Johnson Holy Rock

Oglala Sioux

Pine Ridge Reservation, South Dakota
Interviewed by Joseph H. Cash
Summer 1967

Mr. Holy Rock was the tribal chairman of the Oglala Sioux tribe
and in his forties at the time he was interviewed.

JOHNSON HOLY ROCK I think it's going to take time, much time, to
make our people aware of the importance of time. I remember when Ben
Reifel was here as superintendent; he pounded on this subject of time to
make people time-conscious. But our culture, going way back, is oblivious
of time. The hours in the day are not measured into minutes or seconds.
When the sun rises and sets, that is the span of time within which a person
will do what he wants to do. Whether it's time for the hunt, whether it's
time for the gathering of berries, whether it's time to look at the stars and
moon and make preparations for winter quarters in some area of the
country. Beyond that—to measure time in matters of hours—it just isn't
there. And I think, in just observing my people over the years, that it's
inherited. It's just an attitude of the people. And it's going to take time for
people to perhaps outlive this . . . .

I pointed out that in our rate of progress in terms of years, of decades,
of centuries, we are behind. I said, "We have to have time to also make
our progress . . . ." Even myself, at times I know I've got an appointment to
keep. Well, I'll get there. Maybe a little late, but I'll be there. That attitude
is still part of us. It grows a lot of gray hairs when they first start on a job.
They say, "You show up for work at seven o'clock." Well, if I get there at
seven-thirty, I'm on the job. So what? But for the white man, he figures in
minutes and seconds. You could see the pennies and nickels dropping in
losses. But for the Indian, the value of time just doesn't register.

219

Under strict application, like in the military, the Indian is like a salamander. He can conform because he has to. When he doesn't have to, he's not going to. He reverts back to what he was. I spent three years in the military service. And I spent the first six years of my education under military academy type of schooling. We marched every day, we marched to work, we marched to school, we marched everywhere. We marched before breakfast, and we marched before sundown. And if you stepped out of line, you got court-martialed, just like you would in the Army. So when I was in the Army, it just came as second nature. But when I came back out of the service, time—well . . . .

Keith Jewett

Minneconjou Sioux

Winnebago All-Indian Conference
Winnebago, Nebraska
September 1970

Mr. Jewett is a former tribal police chief at the Cheyenne River
Reservation and is presently a student at the University of South
Dakota. He will shortly assume the leadership of Indian programs
at Midland College, Fremont, Nebraska. He was twenty-eight years
old at the time of this conference.

KEITH JEWETT Our education system is falling down because it's a
white man's education system. And it is through this system that we must
deal. We charge ourselves with better education continuously. But we
always say education is a bad point. Let's do something about it! But
sometimes we don't know how to go about it. It's been suggested throughout this conference that we take some positive steps in the direction of
putting something on for ourselves. And I mean this—it is determination.

Suppose all the people got together and said, "Hey, we want to have
some influence in the education of our children." What if they said that?
What if they got together and said, "We want a school board to represent
us." That's a step in that direction. Then they start putting pressure on and
pretty soon you'll have your different tribal people directly involved in
school board functions. Now this creates a problem because you'll have a
lot of school board members coming from a community where there hasn't
ever been a school board. So now you go into another area. You need
school board workshop sessions. It's a drawn-out thing. Then you learn
something about what your responsibilities are as school board members—
if you want control, if you want determination, if you want direction—
then you have to know what you want these things for and what you
intend to do with it.

221

After we get that done, what comes next? Then we start being dissatisfied. You see, human beings are always wanting more and more and more. I used to sell books, encyclopedias, and I must not have been very good at it, because I'm here. The thing is—we had to keep knocking on doors and keep going, and keep going. We were very positive, we got stronger, we could walk tall to the next door. Invariably there would be an old woman who'd say, "Get the hell out of here, or I'll call the police." So you'd run down the sidewalk and there might be a dog out there. But you still have your deal in your pocket so you don't really care. You run to the next house, and you just keep running.

This is what happens to that theoretical school board that we've created. They've got to do something else. So then they see that they're having input into hiring teachers and things like this. Now they want something more. They want to have something to do with curriculum development. Now they are really getting to be educators. Back there they were nothing. So now we got a lot of lay people who are school members getting involved in education. They want Indian language, which is relatively unheard of until the last year or two. Navajo Community College got it. Now the Indian people in Lower Brule, they want Indian history. So they sit down with the teachers, and they say, "Okay, let's get some recent history books and let's get them with Indian history. Everybody says it's George Washington and the cherry tree. Maybe we've got Red Cloud with the cherry tree also." That's just as important if the students are going to identify with someone.

So that's done—you get involved and say, "Okay, we want that," and you get Indian history whether it's Oglala history or Winnebago history, or whether it's Iroquois history. See, that's a step. The kids are no longer learning about George Washington. Oh, they'll know about him, no doubt, but they'll also know about the great Indian orators of the day. And of course, history. Chief Joseph, Red Cloud, Crazy Horse—fantastic orators. To emphasize this point, I wrote a paper on Abraham Lincoln last semester. And it was a seven-page paper, and for the first three I quoted from a speech of Chief Red Cloud. Everyone in the class, including the instructor, thought it was a quotation from Abraham Lincoln. And after I told them it was Red Cloud, they sat up and listened, because he had something to offer. When these people spoke, they spoke from the heart, because they had wisdom from long years of experience. And they believed this and they spoke. So Indian children can learn of the "Give me liberty or give me death" by Patrick Henry.

But you know this is what the Indian children of today are crying for—"Give me my own direction or don't give me a damn thing." So we can study this, but also we can learn what Indian myths mean. Indianness is a fantastic feature of our culture. And it's important that we think back and we study history with Indian emphasis. Because you can go down to Pine

Ridge and you can see Wounded Knee, and there's a history there—get the feel as you walk around in the valleys and on the prairies. You can feel the presence of something really fantastic in Indian history. You can feel the Oglala, you can go up there around the creeks of Eagle Butte and you can feel Gall with his three wives. You can see that he used to camp along this creek. This is their land, they should know something about it.

After you get this, then you can go into Indian languages. Why should they be forgotten? Why is it in colleges and universities we have to study Hebrew or Latin or Greek or some of the other languages in order to get a Ph.D. when we have hundreds of dialects of the native American language that we can't study? This is the history—this is true American history which goes adjacent with culture.

Reuben Snake

Winnebago

Winnebago All-Indian Conference
Winnebago, Nebraska
September 1970

———————

Mr. Snake was a co-chairman of this conference, which was the first in the nation called in response to President Nixon's self-determination policy. Mr. Snake was in his thirties at the time of this conference.

———————

REUBEN SNAKE   We have a thing going here on Indian brotherhood which I don't think is going to be put down. I think this thing is going to grow. I just told this group over there—they're thinking about meeting your need of having them to come over and talk to you. But they're so wrapped up in important problems that we Indian people have that I told them, "Don't worry about those white people sitting over there. We've stood around patiently for about three or four hundred years. Now let's have them sit and wait a while. We've got something going here that has to be kept going."

Not more than half an hour ago a young Chippewa girl who is a senior in college arrived from Mount Crazy Horse, formerly known as Mount Rushmore, the supposed shrine of democracy, and she has got something going over there. They've been wrapped up in health problems. We've been hearing the cry of the urban Indian over there. So there are several things being generated.

Just before I left the group over there, I said three or four generations ago our fathers didn't get together in council and say, "Well, we've got a number of things to talk over, but I've got a meeting next week and so by sundown tomorrow I'm going to hop on my pony and head out." Indian people didn't do that kind of thing. When they had something to talk about, they sat and talked about it, and they talked about it until

224

they arrived at a consensus of opinion. And whether it took a day, two days, a month—time was irrelevant to them. We say we can't live that way in today's society; we say time is of the essence. I don't know what you've got planned for Saturday and Sunday, but I don't have anything planned. And if my Indian brothers and sisters want to stay here Saturday and Sunday and continue to talk about these problems, I'm going to stay here and talk to them. There are problems so tremendous, so immense, that we can't solve them in three days. We can't leave here at five o'clock with the feeling that we've got something going and we don't have to worry. I think that this conference may well extend over until tomorrow. If things go right, it may carry over until Sunday. And I hope some of you resource people can stick around.

Now just to fill you in a little bit about what is happening in South Dakota. Last May when I first arrived at Rapid City, the Rapid City *Journal* ran a story on the aerial gunnery range, which is part of the Oglala Reservation. In 1942, when this country went to war, the white man was hard put to find land to practice his killing techniques on. One of the best places he could find was Indian land, so he took several thousand acres from the Oglala tribe and said, "We're going to use this until we have perfected our techniques in aerial gunnery and bombing, until we are proficient at killing people. Whenever we win this war, we'll give you your land back." Well, last May in Rapid City, a story came out which said the Government was allowing the Indian people to buy back the gunnery range. Any individual owner of land which was situated on the gunnery range would be given the opportunity to buy back his land. I don't know the exact figures, but I think the per capita income of Oglala people is about eight hundred dollars a year and I don't know how much land you can buy for eight hundred dollars. Well, this story generated some Indian brotherhood movement. A group of Oglala people moved onto the Sheep Mountain Table.

Part of the statement that was publicized was that the Oglalas wouldn't be allowed to buy back all of their land because the United States Park Service needed to enlarge the Badlands National Monument and Sheep Mountain Table was so picturesque that it would have to be included in this national monument. And so the Government wanted Sheep Mountain Table and other acreage to add to the Badlands National Monument.

This kind of thing has been perpetrated against the American Indian for too damn long. The Winnebago tribe is in a fight to save several hundred acres from condemnation by the Corps of Engineers. The Taos Pueblos are fighting for their sacred Blue Lake. Dams, recreation areas, parks—it seems that the best place to build these things is on Indian land.

Well, the protest began at Sheep Mountain Table but it wasn't too well publicized, because Sheep Mountain Table is pretty hard to get to. Only a real hardy Indian can get to it. Not too many white people want to come and listen to what the Indians had to say on Sheep Mountain Table. Weekend after weekend, from May until July, the Oglala people were protesting on Sheep Mountain Table, but it really wasn't getting the kind of recognition that it needed. So a group of them decided, "Why not take our story to the shrine of democracy?" In the months of June, July, and August, 1.6 million people visited Mount Rushmore—tourists from all the fifty states, and from just about every country in the world. They come up there and look at the faces of these four white men who are supposed to be the personification of democracy and brotherhood!

In 1868, the Teton Sioux negotiated a treaty with the United States Government. Part of that treaty said that thereafter any other treaty negotiation had to be approved by three-fourths of the male membership of the Sioux Nation. Some very wise chief saw that this was a way to protect their rights. But in the interim between that and the taking of the Black Hills, this great government of ours found a way to circumvent treaty negotiations. Treaties were negotiated and ratified by the Senate only. And so the Government decided that this wasn't right; that the House of Representatives had to have some say. So there would be no more treaty negotiations, only acts of Congress in dealing with Indian people.

A commission of white people came out to the Black Hills, to the Lakota, got Crazy Horse and some of the other sub-chiefs of the Lakota people drunk, and perpetrated a fraudulent agreement with the Lakota people. Now these people have waited one hundred and two years for payment for the Black Hills. Billions and billions of dollars in timber and gold and other mineral resources in tourism have been realized by white entrepreneurs. The Lakotas too have waited one hundred and two years for some kind of payment to be forthcoming for these Black Hills which are sacred to them. This was sacred land. When I go out into the white community and I negotiate for a new car or home or refrigerator or gas range or something of this nature, I have to sign an agreement—a contract. I agree to pay so much money per month for what I have signed, because I don't have the kind of money to lay down and say, "Here's five hundred bucks for a new refrigerator or stove." I have to deal on the installment system. Now, whenever I don't pay up, my wages are garnisheed or that thing is repossessed.

This is what the Indian people finally decided to do in South Dakota. A group of young Indian people waited for a hundred and two years for the first installment. Now how patient can we be? So we decided to take a little action on repossessing the land. I was up on that mountain. Several times I heard many people make comments pro and con. Many people say, "What the hell do these Indians want now; don't they get enough from Uncle Sam?" Other people say, "Look, we're not prejudiced, but you're making us that way." On the other hand, people have said, "You know, I'm ashamed to be here. I didn't realize that these kinds of atrocities were being perpetrated against your people." One gentleman told me, "I've been coming up here every year for better than twenty years. I've always found it inspiring before." He was from New York or someplace back East. He said, "It's always meant a great deal for me to be here. I'm actually sick now to know that the Government can't deal fairly with your people."

So that's the kind of brotherhood thing that many Indians are generating. I can move into different kinds of roles. I've been a militant, I've been a supermilitant. I helped lead a boycott against a bunch of racists in this part of Nebraska last year. I helped organize a fight to save our Winnebago lands. I was up on Mount Rushmore. I can play that role pretty well. But I feel also that something from this kind of conference can be of benefit to our Indian people. We want to work with you—those of you who are in power positions—in the Government, in political circles, in our universities and colleges that are supposed to be turning out good citizens of our country. I want to sit down and talk to you man to man.

We don't want to come begging any more. We don't want to come with our hand out, pleading for help. We've lived through several centuries of that—that has to stop. We want to stand and talk to you face to face, man to man, and say, "Look, this is what your society has done to us. This is what your kind of culture has perpetrated on us, and we want to work with you to change." This is an Indian brotherhood conference. Indian brotherhood means a lot of things. It means respect, understanding, trust, faith. When that pipe was smoked the other day, it meant that we were entering into a sacred bond with everybody here. We are trying to present to you what we feel are our problems. We don't want you to say, "Well, you know, gee, I'm concerned about your problems, but I don't know what I can do about it." That's happened to us time and time again. Regardless of what position you hold, whether you're in the university or whether you're in government, or wherever you're at. You know, try to say something positive and try to act positively. Don't say, I don't know what I can do for you. We wouldn't have invited you here if we didn't think you could do something for us. Like I said, I'm not much of an orator but these are some of the things that are happening over there.

And I think if that young lady comes over here—I told you she was going into her last year of college, or she's a senior in college, I don't know whether she wants to go on after that or not. She's willing to put that aside for a year to fight for what she believes in—a young girl twenty years old. She has legal custody of her younger brother; she said she's been threatened already by the welfare system that she'll lose that guardianship of her brother if she stays up on that mountain.

A picture of three Indian singers was run in the Rapid City *Journal* last week. The day after that picture ran, one of those Indian men had his house condemned. He had been living in a substandard house for I don't know how long, paying eighty dollars a month rent. But he was a good

Indian; he didn't stand up and tell it like it was, so his landlord just took the eighty dollars a month and let him live in a dump. But when he got up there with his Indian brothers and said, "I'm going to fight for my life in this way, the only way I can, to sing for my people," then his house was condemned and he is without a home. That kind of thing has got to stop. It's going to stop. So all of you people who are here to help us, we ask you to have a little patience. You know all of these problems didn't just happen to us in a day. They've been laid on us for years, for centuries.

A part of the problem was that Indian people were being forced against one another by the influx of white people. For a long time we didn't trust one another. That system still sort of operates. When Uncle Sam has a few coins, he dangles them in front of us and we all fight for them.

It's this way with our black brothers, too, and our Chicano brothers. When Uncle Sam has something to offer, then he throws his black, brown, and red brothers into conflict, fighting for it. That kind of thing has to stop. This brotherhood feeling is here today; it's been here for three days. We're here trying to work together. We want to work with you, but I've just been up here trying to tell you the kind of feelings that are running through most of our Indian people here today. There are pros and cons.

A number of middle-class Indians have put it down. And that's the kind of Indian that does put it down—people who have gained security, people who have got it made, people who have become assimilated, more or less. I think Mr. Brightman really laid it on them when he said, "Those aren't Indians, those are apples, red on the outside and white on the inside." It's the people that don't have it that do this kind of thing—the people that don't have an education, the people that don't have good housing, the people that don't have good health, the people that don't have jobs. All they've got is their bodies. That's all they have to fight the system. And that's why we see these kinds of things happening.

I was on Mount Rushmore the second day that the Indian people took the mountain. I shouldn't call it Mount Rushmore, it's been renamed Crazy Horse Mountain. I was up there. I could see the eagles flying. Eagles are sacred to the Indian people. Indians read signs into things such as these. And it moved me a great deal to see them. So I think what is happening up there is right—right for our Indian brothers and sisters.

I felt that same kind of feeling two days ago when Mr. White smoked the pipe. That kind of feeling is here, too. So I'm asking you to be patient, and while you're being patient, think positively. When these people come back here with their demands, when they come back here please don't get up here and say, "Well, I don't know what power, what authority I have, I don't know how I'm going to help you." Get up here and say, "Well, whatever I can do to help you, I'm going to do." Commit yourself to that and we'll all go away from here feeling a lot better.

Louis R. Bruce

Oglala Sioux-Iroquois

Pierre, South Dakota
National Tribal Chairmen's Association Meeting
April 23, 1970

Mr. Bruce is presently Commissioner of Indian Affairs and is the chief executive officer in the attempt to further Indian self-determination.

LOUIS R. BRUCE   I pleaded for cooperation between us all, and all of you know how much I've talked about this. And I'm so encouraged by this beginning, because today we need to look at some very critical things involving Indians—BIA, water, natural resources—all the way down the line. We should have the chance to sit down and see where we want to go. Regarding the revenue sharing—where do we want to be in that? Do we want to get $25 per head? Where do we end up? Do you want funds to go through the state? Where do we end up? Do you want the funds to go directly to Indians? Well, get busy and do something about it, because it's being worked on and planned now. Where do you want the Bureau to be? I need to know what you want—where you want the education department of the Bureau. Do you want it scattered here, or in HEW? Do you want it separate? Do you want a national Indian board of education? What do you want?

We've got a start. We've got people—you folks—tribal chairmen. I can talk to you, take your advice, suggestions, and recommendations, which I've been pleading for.

Dallas Chief Eagle

Rosebud Sioux

Pierre, South Dakota
National Tribal Chairmen's Association Meeting
April 23, 1970

Mr. Chief Eagle is the author of several books published in America and abroad concerning his people; chief among these is *Winter Count*.

DALLAS CHIEF EAGLE   We desire intensely to belong to the American dream. And you want to be proud of your contributions, not only to your own people but to this country and the world. A democratic form of government did not originate at Jamestown or Philadelphia. It was patterned after the Iroquois Six Nation Confederacy. Not only the eastern tribes but clear across the continent—tribes governed themselves in this manner. The head chief in tribal, band, or even clan rule was parallel in stature and authority to the President. The subchiefs were parallel to the Senate. The council was equal to the House, and underneath this council were the clans and societies. They forgot to project to the European world that this was patterned after the American Indian.

The area of medicine—two-fifths of the medicine that you use today originates from North and South American Indians. Over three hundred years ago, thousands were dying of the festering plagues in Europe. And a phenomenal thing happened. Over an eighteen-year period, over two dozen new vegetables came into Europe, changed the diet of the European world, and served as a strong antibiotic against the festering plague. These are just a fraction of your contributions to the world. And you have much more to contribute—particularly to our Indian people across this country.

You know, in Europe the past week, even in Japan last year when I was over there, they say that because of the American Indian philosophy, his theology, his metaphysical culture, the American Indian has the solution to world peace. So I'm proud.

230

Lehman Brightman

Oglala Sioux

Talk Given at University of South Dakota
Vermillion, South Dakota
February 1970

Mr. Brightman is editor of the *Warpath,* president of United Native
Americans, and a lecturer at the University of California. He is
recognized as one of the leading "militant" Indian spokesmen
in the United States. He was in his thirties at the time of this
interview.

LEHMAN BRIGHTMAN There comes a time in every man's life when
he's got to stand up for what he believes in and be a man, and in women's
lives when they have to stand up and be a woman. Sometimes it hurts,
and you don't want to do something, but you know it's right, and it has to
be done. And it's damn time we quit being silent. We've been silent.
They've put out this thing—the "noble stoic silent Indian who never raises
his voice"—and they have stolen every goddamn thing except the clothes
on our backs from us. And the only way we're going to stop this is to speak
up and become more aggressive. Let them know we have problems; en-
lighten the youth and bring about some change.

Cato Valandra

Brule Sioux

———◆———

Mr. Valandra spoke the following words at the Rosebud Sioux
Tribe Historical Conference on May 4, 1968.

———◆———

CATO VALANDRA   We're going to use your brains and your money
and we're going to raise ourselves to your level—and maybe a little bit
higher.

Appendix I

The Narrators

ANTOINE, Lawrence

BRIGHTMAN, Lehman

BRUCE, Louis R.

CHIEF, Henrietta

CHIEF EAGLE, Dallas

CHILDS, Lucille

CUMMINS, John

CUNEY, Merri Pat

DELORIA, Father Vine

DUBRAY, Alfred

FOREMAN, Clarence

GARRY, Ignace

GINGWAY, Lawrence

GOODBIRD, Titus

GOOLSBY, Celina

HERMAN, Jake

HOLY ROCK, Johnson

JEWETT, Keith

KEEBLE, Jonas

KILLS IN SIGHT, George

LAWRENCE, Levi

LUNDERMAN, Dorothy

MCKENZIE, Frank

MICHAEL, Mitch

MORRISON, Robert

O'CONNOR, Bill

ONE FEATHER, Gerald

OWEN, Amos

PICOTTE, Paul

PROVOST, Cecil

RAINWATER, Purcell

RED STAR, Henry

REIFEL, Ben

ROBERTSON, Paul

ROBERTSON, Sam

ROUBIDEAUX, Antoine

ROUBIDEAUX, Ramon

SAUL, John

SCHUNK, Harold

SMITH, George

SNAKE, Reuben

SNAKE, Sterling

SPOTTED TAIL, Steve

STINSON, Mildred

STRICKER, John

TAYLOR, Nathan

TRUDELL, Mabel

VALANDRA, Cato

WALKER, Neola

WHITE, Felix

WHITE, Noah

WRITER, Sam

Appendix II

The Interviewers

ROBERT CARRIKER Spokane, Washington. Assistant professor of history at Gonzaga University; author of *Fort Supply*; Ph.D. in western history (University of Oklahoma).

JOSEPH H. CASH Vermillion, South Dakota. Associate professor of history at University of South Dakota; director of American Indian Research Project; Ph.D. in western history (University of Iowa).

STUART W. CONNOR Billings, Montana. Archaeologist and practicing attorney; formerly with FBI.

RAMON I. HARRIS Vermillion, South Dakota. Associate professor of history at University of South Dakota; assistant director of American Indian Research Project; specialist in ancient history (University of California at Los Angeles).

HERBERT T. HOOVER Vermillion, South Dakota. Associate professor of history at University of South Dakota; research associate for American Indian Research Project; Ph.D. in western history (University of Oklahoma).

M. EDWARD MCGAA Saint Paul, Minnesota. Attorney; captain, U.S.M.C.; fighter pilot in Vietnam; assistant to the director of Indian education in Minnesota; Oglala Sioux.

Index of Proper Names

Subject Index